THE LIFE AND LOVES
OF A HE DEVIL

From his varied career to his beloved dogs to Ireland, once a place that felt stifling but that now is home, Graham Norton shows how life isn't simply a series of dates and events: it is who and what we love. And so he tells of the men he has loved and lost; the booze that has flowed freely — sometimes with startling results; of his love affair with New York, and the divas who have awed him with their power and imperfections. Here, he shares an amazing variety of experiences, from the mundane (falling asleep on the night bus), to the grotesque (vomit-covered socks), to the sublime (floating down the river singing with Dolly Parton) — a plateful of life stories, along with a dollop of 'Graham Nortonness' on the side.

SPECIAL MESSAGE TO READERS

THE ULVERSCROFT FOUNDATION
(registered UK charity number 264873)
was established in 1972 to provide funds for
research, diagnosis and treatment of eye diseases.
Examples of major projects funded by
the Ulverscroft Foundation are:-

- The Children's Eye Unit at Moorfields Eye Hospital, London
- The Ulverscroft Children's Eye Unit at Great Ormond Street Hospital for Sick Children
- Funding research into eye diseases and treatment at the Department of Ophthalmology, University of Leicester
- The Ulverscroft Vision Research Group, Institute of Child Health
- Twin operating theatres at the Western Ophthalmic Hospital, London
- The Chair of Ophthalmology at the Royal Australian College of Ophthalmologists

You can help further the work of the Foundation
by making a donation or leaving a legacy.
Every contribution is gratefully received. If you
would like to help support the Foundation or
require further information, please contact:

THE ULVERSCROFT FOUNDATION
The Green, Bradgate Road, Anstey
Leicester LE7 7FU, England
Tel: (0116) 236 4325

website: www.foundation.ulverscroft.com

The winner of seven BAFTA awards, Graham Norton is one of the best-known faces on British television. His long-running and ever-popular Friday night chat show, *The Graham Norton Show*, continually features some of the world's biggest stars. Since 2009 he has presented the *Eurovision Song Contest*. He also charms Radio 2 listeners each week on his Saturday morning show.

GRAHAM NORTON

THE LIFE AND LOVES OF A HE DEVIL

Complete and Unabridged

CHARNWOOD
Leicester

First published in Great Britain in 2014 by
Hodder & Stoughton
London

01/16

First Charnwood Edition
published 2016
by arrangement with
Hodder & Stoughton
An Hachette UK company
London

A catalogue record for this book is available
from the British Library.

ISBN 978-1-4448-2744-6

Published by
F. A. Thorpe (Publishing)
Anstey, Leicestershire

Set by Words & Graphics Ltd.
Anstey, Leicestershire
Printed and bound in Great Britain by
T. J. International Ltd., Padstow, Cornwall

This book is printed on acid-free paper

For Rhoda — the be all and end all

Contents

Introduction

It started with a bad oyster. Weeks of planning lay in ruins as I hugged my toilet, hoping that the great god of food poisoning would just put me out of my misery.

The preparations for my fiftieth birthday had got a bit out of hand. What I had imagined would be a drink with a few friends had somehow grown into an enormous gay wedding where I would declare my undying love for myself. Caterers had been booked, menus tasted, cocktails selected, flowers were being unloaded out of the back of white vans, k.d. lang was booked to perform. Now it appeared that unless the whole shindig was relocated to my bathroom, the only thing that would be missing was the host. Too late to cancel, I pressed my face against the cool porcelain and prayed I might feel a little better by that evening. Too sick to present my Radio 2 show that morning, word was spreading amongst the guests that something was up. It is more difficult than you might imagine to write upbeat texts reassuring people that everything is still on, when lying on the floor with stomach cramps and a vomit-stained dressing gown.

By the time the sun had set and I needed to get ready, I had at least stopped being violently ill. I would go to the ball after all. Feeling like an understudy for the real me, I sat very carefully in the back of a taxi as it found its way to Covent

Garden. The party organisers had done an extraordinary job and the venue looked amazing. I felt I had cheated the flowers — they should have been at the Oscars or at the announcement of a Nobel Peace Prize, not the birthday bash of some television presenter. Even the guests as they walked in looked as if they were going to something a lot better than my birthday party.

Looking back, I can finally find it in my heart to say thank you to that oyster. Thanks to that dodgy bit of shellfish I can remember the whole event, didn't embarrass myself and ended the evening tucked up in bed with a mug of peppermint tea. It wasn't how I had imagined my fiftieth birthday would be, but actually I had a fabulous night.

Stone-cold sober, I had stood on the stage to introduce my favourite singer of all time. Almost thirty years earlier some Canadian friends had dragged me to see her perform in a pub in Putney. I had fallen in love with k.d.'s voice that night and soon afterwards, the rest of the world had too. Now she was singing to me for my birthday; in the crowd were the same friends who had introduced us decades before. I looked out at the 300 faces and saw my life reflected back at me. People I liked, people I loved, people I had shared half a century with. My mother and sister, school friends, people I had worked with in restaurants, the gang from drama school, friends from radio and TV, theatre folk, a smattering of chat-show guests, and the friends I get drunk with. All the stories of my life were together in that one room and it made me very happy.

The idea of this book began to grow.

It had been ten years since I'd last written a book and I knew I fancied writing another one. The first had been a fairly straightforward autobiography following the ' . . . and then this happened' pattern. I knew I could have written about the last decade but, looking around the room at my party, I saw what my life really was. It was made up of my passions: Ireland, which I had fallen back in love with; all the people who had helped build my career; my friends from New York who had flown in specially; the men I had loved and lost; the music that had shaped my life; and the booze that was flowing freely. The only thing missing was my dogs.

It seems to me that we are all made up of the things we adore, and by telling my stories through the prism of my passions I hope you will get an insight into my life.

It is a weird experience writing about yourself and while this book is definitely all about me, I was able to pretend while writing it that I was really dealing with a variety of topics. For me this book has been an eye-opener in a way that a simple autobiography never was. I see so many more patterns in my life this time — strange connections and often mysterious bookends emerged as I linked various phases of my life through the things I love.

In order to get some of the dates and facts for this book, I sometimes had to refer to various websites that record aspects of my career and life. There I found the lists of shows I've done, where I was born, who I had dated, the awards

I've won and the money I've earned, but that
wasn't my life. I didn't see myself in those lists of
details. We live in our stories, and the best stories
go on. Funerals see the end of a life but at the
party afterwards, it is like a form of resurrection:
the person we have just said goodbye to is back
in the room as people share their tales.

The stories in this book are a mixed bag.
Fingers crossed you'll find some of them funny,
but there are tears along the way as well. I hope
that you'll also share some of my passions. They
are a fairly broad spectrum of things so even if
one doesn't really float your boat, hopefully
you'll find another that puts wind in your sails.
In an ideal world you'd like dogs, booze, men,
divas, Ireland, New York and work as much as I
do but, most of all, I really hope you like this
book.

1

Dogs

Depressed? Feeling down? Got the blues? Before you head off to the man in a white coat to get a fistful of happy pills, why not consult Dr Norton? Here's my prescription: take two dogs, add a deserted beach on a gusty winter's day, and then unleash the hounds. Watch them galloping towards the waves, ears flapping in the breeze, tongues hanging out of their mouths like pink socks on a washing line, and while it may not cure everything that ails you, things will feel a great deal better. Tears shed into warm fur, a sofa alive with the soft buzz of animals snoring — dogs take you out of yourself and remind you how simple life can be. Complicated feelings rarely are, and nothing underlines that more effectively than the cool draught of a wagging tail.

It doesn't matter how often I remind myself 'they're just dogs', the emotional bond with my fur babies is profound and, as crazy as it seems, fully reciprocated. If you are one of those people who don't 'get' dogs, then I would start flipping pages rather quickly. Or maybe, just maybe, this chapter will change your mind.

The first dog I remember entering my life was Smokey. He was a Keeshond, a small husky-like dog distinguished by black circular markings around the eyes, as if they had just stopped the sled and popped some glasses on to check the map. Oddly, they aren't from the polar wastes at all — they are originally from Holland and bred as barge dogs, though I'm not sure what makes them, or indeed any dog, especially suited to life on a canal.

Knowing my mother, I suspect the arrival of Smokey was nothing to do with her. She is of the old school when it comes to being house-proud. We never doubted how much she loved us but there were certainly occasions when we felt she would have chosen a clean, undisturbed antimacassar over me and my older sister, Paula, running around the house with jammy fingers and a careless crayon. Left to her own devices, I imagine the sofa would have still been wrapped in plastic and all shoes left outside. Coasters matter!

Doubtless our first pet was thanks to my father, who could be sold anything, whether he wanted it or not. He worked for Guinness Brewery as a travelling sales rep so presumably he bumped into guys in pubs who quickly realised that they had an easy mark. I was never there but I imagine most of his ill-judged purchases were in some way designed to make my sister and me happy: 'Your kids will love it!' Ireland in the mid-sixties was going through an epic amount of change. The life we were living as children bore no similarity at all to the one my father had led twenty years before: he had followed horses ploughing fields and drunk milk still warm from the cow; we were growing up in a world of television, pavements and back gardens. Once we graduated beyond playing 'Peek-a-boo', we were a constant source of mystery to him. These greasy-haired mid-afternoon drinkers were selling my dad the secrets of being a modern father. He was a sitting duck. Amongst the many purchases he arrived home with were a cine camera which he never mastered, a set of never-used left-handed golf clubs, a bright orange record player — 'It's the modern style!' — and, best of all, a ball of grey and black fur.

I can only imagine my mother's pursed lips and steely-eyed expression when Dad opened his coat to reveal a little canine Heathcliff.

Nowadays, when families are considering getting a pet they are urged to research breeds to find a dog that is suitable for their lifestyle, age of children and accommodation. Clearly none of these questions had been asked before Smokey was wrapped in an old cardigan and stuffed into the footwell of the passenger seat in my dad's car. But what did we care? It could have been a three-legged greyhound with a circus of performing fleas on his head and we would have been happy. We had a dog!

There are no photos of Smokey as a pup so I presume he entered our life fully formed. Aged four or five, I could waddle up to him and throw my chubby arms around his neck, so on one very important level he was perfectly suited to being a family dog.

I imagine my parents wondered what could

have led the previous owners to abandon lovely Smokey. Well, the truth will out — and so would our dog. Smokey liked to wander. He liked to wander a lot. We lived in the suburbs of Waterford at the time. It's a small city in the south-east of Ireland and we were amongst the first people to move into a new estate of houses. There was a busy road in front but behind there were abandoned acres waiting for more houses to be built, so no one worried too much when the dog went off on his solo jaunts. At first he wouldn't be gone for too long as the lure of food would drag him back before dark, but when these absences started to last past bedtime, then it was felt something should be done.

It was decided that Smokey would get locked into the outside toilet. (In case you ever meet my mother, I should hastily point out that we also had indoor facilities.) But it was only when we attempted to incarcerate Smokey that we discovered he was the Houdini of the dog world. A Houndini, if you will. Doors were mysteriously opened. Tiny windows left ajar for air proved large enough to squeeze a big dog body through. It was becoming a problem.

A knock came on the door one evening. It was a man claiming that our adorable fluffy playmate had been killing his chickens. Surely not. The family unit shuffled outside to the dog stable-slash-loo to investigate further. Smokey was 'out', but there was no denying the number of feathers on the floor. Money changed hands and the strange man left.

Now this is where memory fails. I know that

Smokey vanished entirely shortly after that, but I'm not sure what happened. Did the foul fowl owner catch him in the act? Did he wander off into the arms of some other children till they too learnt the awful truth that this was just a grifter in a dog suit? Or did my parents send him to that 'farm in the country' that unwanted problem dogs sometimes visit? Obviously, I could ask my mother but part of me prefers not knowing. I like the mystery. We chose his name well — Smokey drifting into our life and then vanishing like fog on a river.

* * *

Once we had tasted the joy of dog ownership, the pups kept rolling in. Trixie was next: a sweet Cairn terrier who was the perfect family pet and probably the dog I became closest to. My sister Paula, in order to be educated alongside other nice Protestants, had gone off to boarding school, so for long swathes of time it was just Trixie and me.

I remember we went as a family up to the bright lights of Cork by now, my dad's job had brought us to Bandon, a small town in West Cork to inspect the litter of newborns. When I see puppies I understand those women who become addicted to having babies. Dogs are great but there is something about the touch and feel of a pup. Their hot little bodies, silky coats and happy faces produce an extraordinary and addictive high.

With difficulty we chose one and brought her

home. By now we must have had a book on dog care — perhaps someone had sold it to my father in a pub — so we left Trixie that first night with a hot water bottle and a ticking clock. We weren't training her up to be a suicide bomber, simply trying to give her comfort on her first night away from her mother and siblings. There must have been some issues around house-training but, of course, I was a kid so none of that bothered me. As far as I was concerned, Trixie only existed for my amusement or to help get me out of scrapes.

My mother, after endless nagging from me, had begun to give me very occasional mugs of weak, milky instant coffee. Of course I was only interested in the air of adult sophistication it gave me to sit at the kitchen table — I too could be just like my mother and her friends, swapping gossip on a Friday morning in their favourite local haunt, The Coffee Nook. I would stir it till it went cold and then have to find some way to get rid of it. I wasn't going to drink it — it was disgusting! Mostly I was able to sneak it into a sink or toilet because to not drink it would have resulted in a charge of 'waste' — not a word anyone wanted to hear coming out of my mother's mouth. One day, I got trapped in my bedroom with a mug of the beige, cold liquid. If my mother came in and found it, I might lose my coffee privileges entirely. No sink, basin or bowl at hand, what could I do? Step forward my trusty companion Trixie. I offered her the mug and she apparently had been waiting her whole life to be offered cold, weak instant coffee. She lapped it up with huge enthusiasm, plunging her little muzzle deep into the cup to get every last drop. Delicious.

My mother came into the room. 'Did you drink that coffee?'

'Yes, Mum,' came my angelic reply.

Satisfied, she picked up the mug to go downstairs, Trixie at her heels. About an hour later, I heard a very loud 'Oh my God!' coming from the kitchen. This was big — something had happened. Growing up in my Irish backwater this was very rare, so I raced to see what had caused the commotion. When I got to the kitchen door I stopped and stared. It looked like a pressure cooker of shit had exploded. It seemed unbelievable that so much poo could have come out of one little dog, but our eyes and noses confirmed it to be true.

'What did that dog have to *eat?*' my mother roared at no one in particular.

Much as I loved playing detective, I had no

intention of solving this particular mystery. I shrugged my shoulders and made a mental note for future dog ownership: coffee is not suitable as a canine treat.

When Trixie was about five or six my parents told us they were going to Canada for five weeks. My father had just taken early retirement and my mother had always wanted to visit relatives who had emigrated. This was their chance.

Up till this point in our lives, holidays had always involved cars and caravans, so this was as if they had announced they'd signed up to Richard Branson's flights into space. We were in shock. My sister and I were to stay at school as boarders, and little Trixie was going to spend the time in kennels. It would be a long time for our family pet, but Paula and I would be able to walk from school a couple of times a week to visit her. It seemed like a good plan, but we hadn't factored in the workings of the canine heart.

Boarding school might not have been fun exactly, but at least it kept us busy. I confess I don't remember missing my parents at all, and if I did, the excitement at the arrival of postcards bearing colourful stamps and pictures of snow-covered mountains more than made up for it.

Trixie proved a more sensitive soul. The kennels were perfectly nice and the people who ran them kind, but there were no opportunities to fall asleep in a patch of sun on the carpet or get corners of buttered toast from my mother as she cleared up after breakfast. Our dog went into a decline. Visiting was awful. Trixie had stopped eating and was becoming very weak. She was always delighted to

12

see us but, in retrospect, maybe those sudden appearances didn't help as they gave her hope that her imprisonment was at an end.

The long walk back to school would be a grim affair with tears streaming down our faces, and Paula and I feeling completely helpless. Mum and Dad were on the other side of the world while our side of it was falling apart. Trixie with her dark muzzle and deep chestnut eyes had always had an air of seriousness, but now there was something accusatory in those eyes every time we said goodbyes.

Somehow Trixie survived until our parents came back, but she was never the same again. She had developed a painful, hacking cough that might have started as some sort of kennel cough but soon became a full-blown lung infection, and she wasn't strong enough to fight it. I remember one night near the end. My parents had gone to bed and I was kneeling by the chair Trixie was sleeping on near the Aga. Outside all was inky stillness. It was just us two.

Trixie was in obvious distress as the painful coughing fits pounded her fragile, bony frame. I tried to comfort her and, through sobs, made all sorts of pacts with a God I still believed in, if only he would help my helpless furry friend.

The omnipotent one remained silent, but the vet said nothing could be done.

I remember my father coming home alone. There had been no last-minute miracle or reprieve. I heard him say to my mother: 'I just had to leave. I was afraid I would make a fool of myself.' His eyes were red and I realised this giant of a man had been felled by his love for a tiny dog. It seemed so unfair that he couldn't join the rest of us and openly weep for our loss. We knew he cared just as much as us, but those were the cruel rules of being a man.

People say that it is somehow beneficial for children to experience loss through the death of a pet when they are growing up. Really? I would cope less well, hurt more, every time a friend, a loved one, a parent passed away just because I didn't see my father carry a small, spluttering bundle out of the back door? I suppose it did teach me that life could be cruel beyond all comprehension, but surely that is a lesson we will all learn eventually. Why the rush?

⋆ ⋆ ⋆

No one was in a hurry to replace Trixie, so we took a break from dog ownership after that. By the time there was a new arrival, I was heading off to university. It didn't strike me at the time, but I'm guessing that Bing, a black and white Shih Tzu with his tiny pink tongue permanently sticking out, was somehow meant to replace me. He was very much my mother's dog, as was her final dog (so far!) — a West Highland terrier called Proby.

Calling a Shih Tzu Bing may have a whiff of casual racism about it but, in fact, my mum always said he was named after Bing Crosby, her all-time favourite crooner. To call any dog Proby seemed much harder to fathom.

Bing had been dead for a couple of years and

my father was in a nursing home, and a dog was seen once more as a good idea — company around the house for our mother, and a good excuse to get some exercise. My sister got a call from a friend. There was an older dog that needed a home. His name was Proby. My sister said yes and called our mother to break the good news.

'Proby? What sort of name is that?' We are very accustomed to my mother receiving good news by focusing on the negative — she comes from the 'All silver linings are attached to a bit of cloud' school of thought.

'I don't know, but that is his name and he's too old to have it changed now.' My sister put down the phone.

The next day Paula went to pick up our new family member. A nice lady opened the door and produced the dog. 'Here's little Toby.'

'What?' My sister was momentarily confused. 'I thought — ? Well, great, thanks!' and off Paula went.

We will never be sure if it was the phone line or if one or both parties had been on the wine, but there was no way my sister was going to confess. The dog didn't seem to mind and lived out the rest of his years quite happily until he fell asleep after lunch one day, sprawled out in his favourite spot, and simply never woke up.

If my mother were the sort of woman to give dogs gravestones it would have said 'Proby'. And the secret would still be safe had not Paula stupidly confessed to me and I foolishly assumed, about a year ago, that my mother must already know. Unfortunately, as I told the story to some friends, I realised I was breaking the news to her as well. She took it quite well and my sister is still alive.

* * *

After I left home, my love affair with dogs didn't wane but I never felt I was in a position to be a dog owner. Instead, I became that annoying person who made a fuss of dogs in the street, or, if I visited someone with a dog, they would get all my attention. When I started to earn some money I began to collect dog art — anything with a dog on it, and I would probably want it. I was at a charity auction once where nothing was selling and if it did, the bids were low. My friend, Tim, turned to me and whispered, 'Idiots! If they only knew all they had to do was doodle a dog on a napkin and you'd pay a fortune!' I can't promise that he wasn't right.

An actual flesh and fur dog didn't enter my adult life until 2004. I was dating Kristian at the time. I adore Kristian and I'm sure he'll show up elsewhere in this book but, and I think even he would agree with this, he wasn't a great boyfriend. We met in his native New York but by 2004 he was living with me in London.

Unable to work as a waiter, a pop star, or anything, in fact, boredom had taken hold. He had mentioned getting a dog over the years but I knew it wasn't a good idea. I was busy and Kristian could hardly look after himself — I would have feared for the future of a pot plant left in his care.

In early January Kristian and I were having dinner with one of my oldest and dearest friends, the actress and writer Maria McErlane. She was one of the few of my friends who understood my relationship with Kristian and was keen to help make it work. The subject of a dog came up again. I knocked it down. This time, however, Maria picked it up again. In her pop psychology brain she had decided that giving Kristian something to look after and having something to think about other than himself would be the making of the man. She fanned the flames of the crazy idea and before I knew it, my whole world was ablaze.

I couldn't fight it and so I embraced it: 'Well, I do love labradoodles.' I still knew it wasn't a practical plan, but then Kristian said a very sensible thing: 'If you want something, you make it work.'

Within two weeks we were driving through dull, grey Sunday countryside towards Coventry, making our way down little lanes that had never troubled the screen of a sat nav, but we eventually found the breeder. On the journey, I tried to manage expectations: 'Remember, we don't have to get a puppy today.' Silence. 'We should probably talk to some other breeders.' The hedgerows went past in a blur. 'Our house isn't ready for a dog yet.' I might as well have been the crazy person on the docks urging people not to board the *Titanic*. This was happening.

The bitch turned out to be a fairly short-legged golden Labrador and that gave me hope — I didn't fancy a dog that was too enormous.

17

We followed the mother into a small, brightly lit room with a mixture of straw, newspapers and puppy pee on the floor, and there they were: a puppy pile of such excruciating cuteness you just wanted to stuff all of them into a sack, take them home and fall asleep with them chewing your hair.

Kristian's dad was a vet and much to my surprise, Kristian suddenly came into his own, asking all the right questions and checking the puppies. His father had said to always pick the boldest pup because they would probably be the healthiest and strongest. There was a clear front-runner but I worried that he was already a handful — even though he could scarcely fill my hand yet. I feared for the future, but I kept looking at the size of the mother. She was manageable. We compromised and picked a pup that seemed a little less boisterous. Given what that grew into, I often think of the family who chose the first one — I imagine them surveying the rubble of their home and settling various lawsuits with neighbours.

As we were carrying our gay fur baby back to where we had parked the car, I heard a flesh-tremblingly deep bark and suddenly, from behind a half-stable door, there jumped up a standard poodle so big you could have thought it was a farmhand having a bad reaction to the moon.

We both jumped back.

'Oh, that's the father,' explained the breeder. My heart sank.

The puppy happily curled up in Kristian's lap and we started the long drive home. Somewhere on that journey he became Bailey. Kristian's idea — he was full of them! That night he slept in our bedroom but on the floor and after that his bed was kept in the kitchen. I was going to be the strict disciplinarian. This dog was going to be perfectly behaved.

A puppy trainer was employed. A strict, stocky woman. I would never make the joke that she looked like a lesbian but she was in fact a lesbian. I'm sure that over the weeks that she worked with him she taught Bailey how to do things — he is still quite good at 'Sit' and 'Lie down' — but, mostly, she seemed to teach him how to love her much more than myself and Kristian — when Bailey saw her, he went hysterical in a way that I have never seen since. I suspected that, uncharacteristically, she must have had a sausage secreted about her person.

★　★　★

It soon turned out that the only thing Bailey was truly gifted at was growing. Every morning he seemed a little bigger. If you popped out for a pint of milk and came back, he seemed to have grown. I'm surprised we couldn't hear his bones straining and squeaking as he transformed from the size of a shoe into a large piece of hungry furniture — think a hairy two-seater sofa with a stomach. In fact, Bailey was so big he seemed to have taken up the human-sized space left by Kristian's departure.

Bad boyfriend had become intolerable boyfriend and no amount of dog care was going to

19

help. With his return to New York, I was left holding the baby but happily Bailey will always provide a link between us. Once the angry scars of the break-up had begun to fade we became friends again and now our phone calls always begin with me looking at Bailey sprawled on the floor like an enormous, tattered hearthrug and exclaiming, 'It's your bad daddy on the phone!'

Labradoodles come in all sorts of shapes, sizes and finishes: it seems the basic process of introducing a poodle to a Labrador is a fairly inexact science. Bailey is at the larger end of the scale, with shaggy Dusty Springfield-style hair in a colour breeders call golden, but which you and I would recognise as blond. An old lady I met while out walking once described him well when she cooed, 'He's like a Disney dog!' And there certainly is something of the cartoon dog about him. Adorable but on the simple side — the sort of dog who drives you to laughter and fury, but very rarely to pride.

It was during the 1980s in Australia that Wally Conron first had the idea of breeding Labradors and poodles, as he wanted to create a guide dog suitable for blind people with allergies. Genius. Now, what he did create was a fabulous, family-friendly pet that looks great in photographs, but there is something about combining the intelligence of a poodle with the simplicity of a Labrador that results in a hungry genius. Given that Bailey would happily launch himself across the M25 if he thought there was half a biscuit on the other side, I'm not sure I'd feel very easy leaving him in charge of a human life. Some labradoodles have, I know, been successfully trained as a companion or an assistance dog for the disabled, but I'm yet to see one in the traditional harness leading a blind person through the busy streets of London town. I have, on the other hand, met at least three people whose labradoodles failed their first year of training for this task and so graduated to being a pet rather than a working professional.

After my initial training with Bailey I felt he was pretty good. He understood basic commands and he came when you called him. I began to take him to big parks and he played happily with the other dogs while I made small talk: 'How old?' 'What breed?' 'Oh, yes, mine does that too.'

Oddly, these conversations very rarely involve me being on television or, indeed, even knowing each other's names. I'm Bailey's dad just as the man I'm talking to is Oscar's owner or the lady who walks Archie. On the dog run we are simply there to hand out treats and put our fur babies on a lead when they are tired.

I enjoyed the anonymity and looked forward to these jaunts. Then the weather got warmer and with the milder temperatures came picnics. Dog owners reading this will immediately know what I mean.

The first incident occurred in Hyde Park. Before I had Bailey I'd seldom walked in the park. Even now when I encounter people out for a walk unaccompanied by a dog, I think they look crazy. As a dog owner you start to notice your fellow park users more. People and their pets — check to see if their dog is on a lead or if it looks like some sort of pit bull. Walk on. People taking a break from the office — often nicely dressed, may have a sandwich. Avoid. Children — difficult this one, because Bailey does look like a giant teddy bear come to life. Sadly, because he is also the size of a Mini Cooper, with paws, the chances of him knocking a kid over are very high. Crying, apologies, angry parents. It's not worth it. Avoid.

Then there are the huge swathes of the population who avoid *you*. To many cultures the idea of having a dog as a pet is filthy and inexplicable. I do understand this. I have visited villages in Africa where dogs are just kept as a form of sanitation in that they eat up all the waste. You might encounter a cow sheltering from the heat in someone's home but never a filthy dog. The same is true of many countries. Shocking, then, for such people to find themselves in Britain where the dog is almost as sacred as the cow is in India. And this was my biggest lesson when it came to Hyde Park: it is used by many Middle Eastern people. I also discovered that they enjoy having large family picnics at sundown. Given the topography of parts of the park, it is often very hard to see what might be nestling over the brow of the next hill. Added to this, the food served at these feasts is typically very aromatic — a dangerous combination.

I learnt this lesson the hard way. One evening, while I was blissfully unaware, Bailey with his finely tuned dog nose was only too certain of the

22

culinary delights that awaited. One minute we were walking along, him sniffing every tree, me surveying the horizon for potential disaster, when suddenly he bolted.

Most people have seen the YouTube clip of the man in Richmond Park impotently screaming for his dog, Fenton, to come back . . . well, I have lived that man's pain. Bailey disappeared over a hill and soon I could hear varied screams. This was not good.

At the brow of the hill I looked down on a sea of carnage. About a dozen people, the women in beautiful saris, were running for their lives while one very happy dog stood on a blanket amidst upturned glasses and plates, gorging himself from a bowl of something delicious.

I retrieved my hound and began the process of apologising. The fact that they were so nice about it only made me feel even worse — if there is any approved etiquette for this situation I don't know it. I was miles from home so they couldn't come back for food; nor were there any food shops on the horizon. In the end I just held out a wad of cash as some sort of compensation but that was waved away. I got the feeling that they were all just grateful to still be alive. Maybe this is how people in Yosemite Park react when the park ranger has removed a marauding bear from their campsite.

Obviously I knew that I was responsible for Bailey's criminal activity but I'm afraid I quickly became the sort of dog owner who blames other people for their dog's bad behaviour. Greenwich Park. It wasn't even a nice day — why were these people sitting on the grass eating chicken? Victoria Park. Chatting to a couple wheeling a stroller. Why would you leave baby rusks in an open bag underneath the pushchair? The final straw was back in Hyde Park. We were on one of the large meadows with a wide range of vision. No one sitting on the ground. Run, Bailey, play! He bounded away and returned moments later with a slice of pizza flopping from his mouth. A smartly dressed woman sitting on a park bench assured me it didn't matter. She was fine. I was furious. Why wasn't she having lunch in a restaurant?

Bailey's original trainer had by now emigrated to the Caribbean to run a bed and breakfast, but I finally admitted to myself that I needed more help. I phoned around and got a highly respected dog trainer. He dressed as if he were on safari or were some sort of mercenary soldier of fortune. I liked it; he meant business. I explained the problem.

Apparently we needed to perfect Bailey's recall (that's your dog coming back when you call it, in civilian speak). The trainer organised the training sessions like some sort of sting operation: one of his assistants would be seated on a blanket 100 yards away eating a sandwich; another day, we started training with great urgency because he didn't want the KFC he'd secreted on a park bench to go cold.

We had several lessons and I liked to think Bailey was improving, but I fear most of that was the figment of a proud father's imagination. One day, as the trainer was packing his paraphernalia of training leads and Tupperware containers filled with treats into his camouflage backpack, he turned to me and said with a sigh, 'I think that's as good as that dog's going to get.' It seemed Bailey had reached his full potential. I now spend nearly all summer every year at my house in Ireland, which has four acres of garden for Bailey to roam in. Whilst I do love Ireland very much, there is at least part of me that is there just to avoid picnic season.

Now please don't misunderstand: Bailey's obsession with being able to eat things isn't just confined to the park. My kitchen is carefully arranged so that anything edible is out of reach. Given that Bailey must be nearly five feet tall when he puts his front paws up on the counter surfaces, this means most things are almost out of my reach too. My petite mother in particular can't bear it because she isn't even able to toast a slice of bread until somebody comes along to get it down for her.

We discovered his love of baked goods early on. My sister Paula had cut herself a slice of brown bread for toast and had her breakfast. A short while afterwards, my brother-in-law Terry came down into the kitchen.

'Where's the bread?'

'On the counter, where I left it,' my sister replied in a way that suggested he was blind. Terry still couldn't see it.

The fate of the bread became clear when Bailey slumped to the floor with a large, loaf-shaped lump protruding from his stomach. Not a crumb was left on the counter. He is as meticulous as he is ravenous.

Dinner parties have become especially difficult because there are so many distractions with people and booze milling about. One night I put a platter of cold meats on the table with a handful of cherry tomatoes on top. I went back to the kitchen to get something and when I returned to the dining room something struck me as different. It took me a moment to realise what. All the meat was gone. Vanished. There just remained the tomatoes, rocking gently on the plate, like the trick where the tablecloth is pulled away leaving the table setting undisturbed.

I'm not completely stupid and have learned to try and avoid these instances, but Bailey is ever watchful for his chance. A group of friends and I were in the garden about to have cheesecake with our coffee when a plane flew very low over the house. We all looked up. I'm not sure to this day if Bailey had managed to bribe a pilot to change his course, but when we looked down again there was an empty plate and a large dog running off with a wheel of cheesecake between his chops. I've lost count of the number of times I've been busy doing something and heard shrieks from my guests as Bailey has nosed his way into a bowl of dip or decided that everyone was finished with the milk in the jug. Last summer I cooked lamb and having served everyone, put the large amount that was left back in the kitchen ready for seconds, carefully shutting the door behind me to prevent a serious case of meat theft. I was clearing some dishes when my mother enquired about the lamb and the whereabouts of Bailey. I explained that everything was fine because I had closed the door. With that, Bailey approached the glass panel of the kitchen door but on the other side of it. A muzzle dripping with lamb juice and a contented look seemed to say, 'Thank you for letting me eat in peace for once.'

★   ★   ★

Given how challenging life with a large, disobedient dog can be, you might well ask the question: 'Graham, why did you get another dog?' Well, let me explain.

Every time I break up with someone I assume I will never have sex again and be single for the rest of my life. Thankfully, thus far, I have consistently been proved wrong.

After Kristian, along came Ben and with him a small Jack Russell called Derek. While my affair with Ben was pretty rocky and short-lived, the same could not be said of Bailey and Derek.

They adored one another and happily played together for hours. It was a fantastic arrangement: I no longer had to hope I bumped into other dogs in the local park as Bailey had a built-in playmate; and when Ben and I went out, I no longer felt guilty about leaving my dog alone, because he had Derek.

To be honest, the relationship with Ben lasted far longer than it should have simply to keep Derek in our lives. Eventually, though, I had to admit defeat and Bailey was left Derekless.

It wasn't a hard decision to look for a permanent companion dog. Looking after two was very little extra work and the benefits were enormous. This time I felt I should do the decent thing and get a rescue dog. I began my search.

Dogs Trust is an amazing charity that has a state-of-the-art facility to the west of London in Uxbridge, with heated floors, large paddocks to play in and wonderful, caring staff. So much so, it is possible to leave there without crying, which is the biggest compliment I can pay them.

I brought Bailey out there and he was matched with a dog he got on with like a house on fire, galloping around the play area like they had known each other all their lives. The problem was this dog was nearly as big as Bailey. Tempted as I was, I knew this was not a good idea. The nice people at Dogs Trust understood, and they went to fetch a smaller option.

It was Derek!

I almost called Ben to see if he had lost his dog but then it became clear that despite his looks, this was a different beast entirely. The two dogs didn't hate each other but after a casual bit of bum-sniffing they simply ignored each other. Again, this wasn't going to help my life. Who knew that Bailey could ever be compared to Cinderella's delicate glass slipper? I needed the perfect fit.

Having been disappointed, I was excited to get a call a couple of weeks later from the staff at Dogs Trust telling me they thought they had the perfect match. Bailey was piled into the car and we headed off for another session of doggy speed-dating.

The potential playmate was a rust-coloured terrier with longish legs, a ridge of hair along her back and a docked tail. For some reason the staff had decided to call her Madonna. I chose to ignore that and we brought them out to the paddock. It was perfection. They ran in circles, rolled around and generally seemed entranced by one another. We had found our companion dog. The only problem I could see was the name. I could not have a dog called Madonna unless I changed Bailey's name to Elton. I compromised and settled on Madge.

Given what I now know about Madge, I marvel at how well she behaved when she met Bailey at Dogs Trust. Since that day she has never encountered another dog she actually likes, so I can only imagine the supreme effort she made in the paddock. It was as if someone had given her a pep talk before we arrived: 'If you do this, if you pretend to be nice for just a little while, then you can get out of here!' She did and she did.

Rescue dogs are special. They are loving and loyal — is grateful too human an emotion to give a dog? — but they are also complicated. Who knows what traumas Madge went through before she found herself in the warm, dry confines of Dogs Trust, but whatever happened, it has left her with quite a lot of issues. She doesn't like men in high-visibility jackets, people on skateboards, noisy trucks, suitcases on wheels, buskers or practically any other dogs. Add to that the normal antipathy towards cats, squirrels and foxes and you have quite a fussy walker. On the plus side, she is wildly affectionate towards people and the obvious bond between herself and Bailey is more than I could have hoped for. Her constant attention and desire to play, which involves biting and pulling his tail, straddling his head or hanging off his ears, has without doubt kept him younger and more active than his ten years would suggest. Madge may have brought new and undreamt-of problems into my life but in terms of doing the job I wanted her for, she has been a huge success.

Being a re-homed rescue dog also tells you something else about their character: they are survivors. About half an hour after Bailey and I welcomed Madge into the back of my car we were at my favourite pet shop on Elizabeth Street in the Belgravia area of London, to get her a nice new lead and collar rather than the yellow, branded ones that she had from the charity. Dogs are welcome in the shop so I was bringing them both in. As I turned the door handle, I somehow lost hold of Madge's lead and, untethered, she skipped off.

As she scampered into the traffic of Elizabeth Street, I imagined the awkward call to Dogs Trust: 'That one's dead already, do you have anything similar?'

Madge may be fearless, but standing in the middle of Elizabeth Street she looked beyond vulnerable. I tried calling her but she apparently didn't know either of her names, and when I stepped closer she moved away. Happily, a passer-by bent down and grabbed her lead. She was going to last another day.

Over the years, Madge has had many close calls. Wandering off for hours in Ireland, chasing horses (she doesn't like them, either) and one particularly trying night when I had to sit up till three in the morning with the front door open waiting for her return as if she were an errant teenager. She was, in fact, racing all around the snow-covered neighbourhood chasing foxes, after she managed to slip out of her collar. As her dainty feet clattered into the hall I was filled with relief and fury: thrilled she was alive, while simultaneously wanting to kill her. It's an emotion every dog owner in the world has experienced.

The closest she has come to departing planet Earth was another midnight escapade. My house in London has access to a fenced garden that backs onto the Thames. One night, before I knew better, I let Bailey and Madge out there for their last wee before bed.

Garden smells are a source of delight to dogs at any time but at night they seem to become

31

more intense. Like a drug addict searching for her next fix, there was no way Madge was coming when I called her. Not wanting to wake the neighbours, my hissed cries of 'Madge!' became more desperate and exasperated. Finally, I made out her shape on a low wall behind some bushes, right by the river. I moved in to grab her but like a phantom she suddenly disappeared. Had I imagined her being there? A moment of silence was followed by a distant splash. She had fallen the fifteen or twenty feet into the freezing, current-filled Thames.

Panicked as I was, I knew not to jump in after her: the news always reports drownings of people who attempt to save their dog from the sea or rivers — invariably they are survived by their puzzled, wet pet.

I started calling her name loudly now, trying to guide her back to the slipway that is the centre of the garden. If she started swimming the other way, I knew there would be no escape route and she would certainly not survive. I made my way to the water's edge still calling and searching the tar-black darkness for some sign of her.

I don't know how much time elapsed but it seemed like at least ten minutes had passed before I noticed something. Was it a piece of wood? I struggled to make it out but finally I could see that it was her tiny head guiding herself towards the shore. At this point it was like a movie. The music soared. I was hysterical with delight. Of course, if it *had* been a movie Madge would have thrown herself ecstatically into my arms and rejoiced at being alive but because it was real life, what actually happened was that she stepped from the river, gave herself a vigorous shake and ran off in search of the same sublime smells that she had been enjoying before this unexpected dip.

Soon, though, she realised how cold and weak she was and followed me meekly into the house. Then came the shaking and shock. I didn't realise until afterwards that shock is the greatest killer of dogs, especially smaller breeds. Their gums go white and unless there is a vet handy there is very little that can be done. I'm glad I didn't understand that night that having got her back from the murky depths of the river, I came just as close to losing her while she shivered in my arms in the kitchen.

Julian Clary once told me that we get the dogs we deserve. I think it is more accurate to say we get the dogs we need. I dread to think how self-obsessed and removed from reality I might have become over the years if it wasn't for my furry friends. After all, it is hard to remain smug and aloof when you are wrestling with two over-excited dogs and struggling to pull a plastic bag out of your coat pocket to pick up a piece of shit. If Bailey and Madge had to explain the world to an alien visitor, I imagine they'd say their poo is like a form of currency or at least extremely valuable, because I insist on collecting every piece they produce. They must be expecting one day to be led into an imposing building fronted by Corinthian columns: The Bailey and Madge Museum of Mess. Fight for a ticket.

I have improved, but when I first started walking the dogs I felt we were in some sort of bubble, and that the things I said to them couldn't be heard by other pedestrians: 'Yes, he is a fat man' 'What ugly children!' 'No, that doesn't fit her, does it?' Perhaps my worst *faux pas* happened after I got a new cleaning lady.

Margaret is from Ghana and being around the dogs doesn't come easily to her. So, in order to prevent them potentially eating her alive, every time she arrives at the house she gives them a dog treat. This is a lovely gesture but, of course, now makes her welcome even more raucous. In short, my dogs truly, deeply love Margaret.

One day, we were passing a local estate agent's office when a very smartly dressed black lady came out of its polished glass and chrome doors. The dogs went wild. Surely this was their favourite woman in the whole world? Understandably, the woman looked shocked at the reaction she had provoked. In an attempt to explain their behaviour, I opened my mouth and found myself saying the following phrase aloud: 'I'm so sorry, but they think you're the cleaner.'

It hung in the air like the offensive smell of old fish. She said nothing and nor did I. There was really no explaining or coming back from what I had said so we simply walked on, leaving a bemused lady standing on the pavement certain that I had raised my dogs as racists.

Now, you might have wondered, given how much I love these two beasts, why they haven't featured more on television. After all, Paul O'Grady is never without a canine co-host; Ben Fogle normally has a dog at his side; and even *Top Gear* featured Bailey's sister for a while.

Believe me, I have tried. I was a guest on the pilot for a Sharon Osbourne chat show and they asked if I wanted to bring Bailey on. He wasn't very old at the time and I figured if I had enough dog treats it would be all right. I was wrong. Turned out, Bailey had a great deal more to say than I did. Sharon and I conducted our chat over a cacophony of barking. I swore never again.

When *The One Show* asked me if I would bring my dogs with me on to the show, I explained that life would be easier if I didn't. I can't remember what went on that day but in the end, I somehow found myself with not enough time to take the dogs home to drop them off before I made my way to the studios. I called and explained. The production team was thrilled.

At this point they had not met my dogs.

Bailey and Madge walked into the green room and duly wagged their tails and accepted treats. Everyone made a fuss of them and I was quietly pleased at how well behaved they were being.

The idea was that I would have a bit of an interview with Adrian Chiles and Christine Bleakely first and then a member of the crew would walk in with the dogs. Simple.

We had our chat and then the camera cut to my dogs. They were straining on their leads, desperate to get to me. Again I was secretly pleased. Then I'm not exactly sure what happened, but I think Madge caught sight of herself in a monitor and assumed it was another dog. As previously noted, she does not like other dogs. She went into a fit of barking and Bailey, being easily led, joined in. All hell broke loose. Bailey jumped onto the couch and started howling. Christine Bleakley was still trying to ask me questions while a dog that was bigger than she was deafened her in one ear. I clung on to Madge's lead while she bounced around the studio like some sort of hairy ginger balloon. Afterwards, a friend said it had looked like one of those occasions when protesters try to take over the news or *Question Time* — doggy revolutionaries seizing their moment in front of the cameras to call their canine comrades all over the UK to take action. Rise up! Free pigs' ears for all! Death to cats! The clip can still be enjoyed on YouTube.

Happily, there were no cameras around one Wednesday morning, about five years ago, when I took the terrible twosome out for their morning walk. On the previous Monday night there had been a gentleman caller and we had done what boys sometimes do. It had been fun, and in the morning I waved him on his way. Back in the bedroom I set about tidying up some of the debris from the night before. (There are some things I don't feel I should expose Margaret the cleaner to.) Things were put back in cupboards and drawers but while I was able to find the ripped foil wrapper, I couldn't see its now used contents anywhere . . . under the bed, in the bathroom bin — it was nowhere to be found. I even texted the man involved to ask him if he

36

knew what had happened to the missing piece of our love puzzle. He didn't. I simply filed it away as one of life's mysteries. Cut to the Wednesday morning in the park. The dogs were doing their normal sniffing around — Madge dashing from one smell to another, while Bailey stood taking in as much as possible from each scent like the person at the gallery who reads every sign at the exhibition. Madge did her business and it was collected and stored carefully in a bin and then, a few moments later, Bailey squatted. I picked up his deposit and got rid of it. When I looked back at Bailey, however, he was now lying on the ground and pawing at the base of his tail. Odd. I went towards him to investigate and as I got closer I was horrified to find that the mystery of the missing condom had been solved. It was hanging out of Bailey's rear end like some long, thin, ghostly finger.

Even worse than seeing it was the realisation that I would have to extract it from him. I grabbed hold.

Now, I always knew they were stretchy but I had no idea to what extent — I seemed to be halfway across the park and it was still attached to a baffled Bailey. I can't begin to imagine what the mothers walking by with their children on the way to school made of the sight that met them that morning: 'Oh, look, it's that man off the telly yanking a condom out of his dog's bottom.' I resisted the urge to inform them that, despite the visual evidence to the contrary, I had not in fact been fucking my pet. If dignity is something that interests you, never get a dog.

Clearly life with two of these creatures is not easy but I do truly believe it is better. Despite all the humiliation and disasters that are associated with owning dogs, there comes stability and boundless amounts of unconditional love. I adore our routine. Most mornings I crawl out of bed, throw on my gym kit, brush my teeth and then wake the slumbering beasts. Having been very strict in the beginning about them not sleeping in my bedroom, they now find themselves there most nights. My excuse was that I could sleep in later because I wouldn't be worried about them down in the kitchen bursting to go out for a wee, but of course the truth is I just enjoy their company. After nearly ten years I'm still entranced by those funny sleep yelps and paw twitches as they chase phantom squirrels in their dreams, while the sound of Bailey snoring spread-eagled on his back has never failed to make me smile. Compare that to lovers where after six months, the tiniest lip smack or grunt while I'm trying to sleep nearly drives me to murder. Maybe it is sad that no human has yet managed it, but these two dogs have tapped reservoirs of love in me that I didn't know I had. I may be single, but there is no doubt in my mind that I have significant others.

2

Ireland

The afternoon was sunny and still. We had finished lunch and moved outside with our drinks and coffees to enjoy the regatta, of which we had a clear view from the garden.

During this annual event, various teams from surrounding villages come together to compete in rowing races while a crowd gathers on the small, bunting-festooned pier to see the action. It's more or less the same every year, the only difference with this one being that the sun had decided to show up for once, instead of the usual driving rain and gales.

From somewhere in the crowd, the announcer's metallic tones were calling out the upcoming events from a cheap speaker attached to a telegraph pole, telling us the winners and commentating on the races. From where we were sitting, his voice was loud and clear as it came across the water.

'And now the results for the ladies' under-sixteens. That race, ladies and gentlemen, was a photo-finish.'

'Ohhhh,' we all cooed. 'How very posh and exciting!'

'So, if anyone took a photograph of the finish of that race, could they bring it to one of the regatta officials at the end of the pier.'

If that had happened in some Hollywood movie portraying life in Ireland it would have seemed patronising and clichéd, but what's so wonderful about my homeland is that the man making the announcement knew that what he was saying was ridiculous but was happy to go ahead and say it anyway. Irish people can never be the butt of the joke because we *are* the joke. We created it, we maintain it and we laugh longer and harder than anyone else.

My father grew up in a tiny village called Carnew in the beautiful wooded county of Wicklow. The stories he told us growing up were almost always about small farmers, the local priests or various well-known characters from the area. You may think you know what the term 'character' means, but bear in mind that once, when I was standing in the Carnew graveyard with my Aunty May and a name on a tombstone caught her eye, she said, 'Oh, now that fella was a real character.' She paused as if to recall all the crazy things he got up to. 'He killed himself.' The joke can get quite dark.

Whenever we visited my father's birthplace as children it seemed incredibly dull: a church, a chapel, a long stone wall which concealed the castle, and buildings that Dad pointed out as having been something marginally more interesting than what they were now. His exotic tales of rural madness didn't seem to fit the place at all: surely this wasn't where the old farmer who wore a vest of rabbit skins had lived? Apparently he had put the fresh skins next to his body and left them on all winter to stay warm. When spring had come, he had found that the untreated furs had grafted themselves onto his own skin and he that could never take them off again. Is that even possible? I doubt it, but as children we loved thinking about his desperate tugging and his sweating, distorted face as he realised the full horror of what had happened.

Some of my father's stories were sweeter. A man had cycled his whole life. You never saw him without his bicycle clips. One day he arrived home breathless, by now an old man. He sat down and said to his equally ancient wife, 'You know, I think that bike of mine is beginning to lose its speed.'

My mother grew up at the other end of the country and in a totally different environment — a small, terraced house that backed onto the railway lines in grimy, industrial Belfast. Her stories were about people being killed in accidents, trips to the movies, and my grandfather leaving the house with a dustbin lid as a hat to protect himself from falling bombs in World War Two.

★   ★   ★

My mother could best be described as a no-nonsense sort of woman. She comes from a time where waste was a sin and emotional outbursts were seen as the worst sort of indulgence. When I was a little boy, there was lots of sitting on her lap and kisses but the wooden spoon was never far away. After just one day of school, I decided it wasn't really for me. I loved my schoolbag and

41

new pencils, but didn't really feel the hours spent at a desk were worth it. My mother begged to differ. Each morning we would set off, me with a satchel of books and my mother with her trusty wooden spoon. As we got closer to the clanging school bell I would hang on to railings to delay my arrival. My mother then swung into action. It was swift but effective. Still dragging my feet and wailing like a defective ambulance, I would be delivered into the arms of my teacher, Miss Costoloe. There are all sorts of modern phrases to describe my mother's style of parenting: tough love, firm but fair, no nonsense. I would simply call it Irish, though my mother must have been quite an extreme example. She was sitting quietly at a meeting of Mothers' Union an organisation a bit like the Women's Institute one evening when she had to listen to another member describe the awful mother she had seen that morning beating her child in the street with a wooden spoon. My mother sank down in her chair while her friends — who knew exactly who it was — suppressed prim, lipstick-framed giggles. While it does sound like I'm describing child abuse, even at the age of four I must have been able to figure out that if I didn't want to be slapped with a spoon I should just go to school. After a couple of weeks I did just that.

Years later, when I was just about to do the equivalent of 'A' level exams in Ireland — the Leaving Certificate — my mother gave me a good luck card. Inside it she had written, 'You can only do your best.' Sweet. Then on the line below: ' . . . but do it!' Oh. Her mothering

42

technique was still intact.

Where the two worlds of my parents came together were in the stories of family secrets and scandals: the girls who went to live in England, the boys who were caught wearing make-up and then killed themselves, the jilted brides, the miscarriages, the forgotten children who had died young and were never spoken of again. As a boy I longed to know more. I would sit as quietly as I could when the grown-ups were speaking in the hope that for a few moments they might forget I was there and let slip some juicy morsel: 'She's at her wits' end with his drinking' 'Apparently the boy she's dating up in Cork is a Roman Catholic' 'You know that isn't her real sister!'

The countryside seemed packed with people living lives that would make depressing short stories or long films with subtitles. The tale of the three unmarried sisters who lived together. I remember driving past their house — a stark, grey box waiting at the end of a long tree-lined drive, the entrance to which was flanked by pillars so close together it seemed unlikely that even the smallest vehicle could come or go. People were talking: it seemed one sister would escape. She was the housekeeper for a local farmer but everyone was aware that their relationship went further than that. She knew that some day soon he would make their love public and do the right thing by marrying her. One morning, however, at the spinsters' breakfast table, another one of the sisters took a rare delight in reading out an engagement notice from the local paper. The farmer was going to marry a widow from the other side of town who owned land. The heartbroken sister ran the half-mile to the farmhouse, not willing to believe that such betrayal was possible . . . but it was. The farmer had gone. She turned and locked the door to the house she had cleaned and cared for and thought one day would be hers. Defeated, she walked dry-eyed back to rejoin her sisters in their barren house where the silence was broken only by sighs and the creaking of stairs. The farmer never came back to the homestead and over the years, the garden grew up to swallow the house and all its contents until now the only sign it ever existed is when a ray of sun penetrates deep into the greenery and there is a little glint from a long unopened window, like the flash of a panther's eye hiding in the darkness.

The atmosphere of secrets and shame made growing up in Ireland seem suffocating. Another person's rural childhood might have involved galloping horses through crashing waves and raising an abandoned fox cub as a pet, but mine seemed to consist of ticking clocks, boiling kettles and drawn curtains. In fact, if I had been writing a book about my passions and loves twenty years ago, I doubt very much that I would have included a chapter on the country where I was born and brought up. Since then, though, we've both changed a great deal. I've grown older and if not exactly wiser, I have at least started to rethink life and see things from a different perspective.

A real turning point in my relationship with Ireland was when my father died. Like a cruel punishment for life crimes he never committed, he ended his days, made helpless by Parkinson's disease, in a bleak nursing home.

When he died, the sense of loss was overwhelming but at the same time we all understood that he hadn't just left us — he had escaped. To no longer have to watch him suffer meant that in death our father could be reborn. Once someone goes, you no longer think of them as the pale, gaunt old man waiting to die; suddenly, he is alive once more in the collective memory and in his prime. The man that could build and carry and dig. The bashful groom, the loving father. The guy we had wanted to live for ever now could, unburdened by a body that had failed him so badly. The other strange thing I discovered is that in death the person you have lost is revealed to you in a way they never could be in life. I had always seen this man simply as my father, but now everyone who came to the house with a bottle of whiskey or a fruitcake also shared their stories. It turned out he wasn't just a dad: he was a friend, a colleague, a joker, a thrill-seeker.

As the funeral approached, in addition to seeing new facets of my father, I was also beginning to fully understand the small community I had grown up in. Living there had stifled me and I spent most of my childhood and adolescence longing to be released. Shaking hands while familiar faces muttered, 'Sorry for your loss' was the classic small-town scene that would have induced a great deal of eye-rolling in the teenage me, but now it provided much-needed comfort. The community had lost one of their own and was coming together to make sure no one stumbled in the gap. The bonds that I had felt holding me back were now there to support me. I liked it.

The theme of leaving is, of course, nothing unusual in Ireland. From Saint Brendan the voyager in the sixth century, to the millions who fled the potato famine and the thousands who still leave every year to find work or excitement elsewhere, the small island on the edge of Europe has given huge swathes of the planet a greenish hue. The difference in the modern world is, of course, that we have the option to return. I've read heartbreaking accounts of the living wakes that were held for people heading off to the new world. Inability to read or write in a time before telephones or aeroplanes meant that leaving was the same as being buried alive, the loved ones left behind certain they would never see you again. Given that that was the choice they made, it gives you some small insight into their levels of desperation.

Opposite Cork airport is a big sign that simply says: 'Welcome Home'. Part of the thinking behind the billboard may be to do with a touristy version of Irish friendliness, but the much more compelling reason for such a statement is simply that it is true. The vast majority of people who visit each year have some family connection, be it immediate or lost in the desolate mists of generations long gone. As I drive away, towards the west, I read it and know that it is speaking to me. I am home. The secret password given, the door opened, and entry to an exclusive club granted.

★ ★ ★

In recent years I have done more than simply return. I have been invited back. This always makes me feel very grown up and is somehow a measure of success that no BAFTA or comedy award can begin to match.

For years my school had chosen to studiously ignore me. Fair enough. I have never made any secret of the fact that my years spent there were far from being the happiest of my life. I wasn't bullied or mistreated in any way, but I never even vaguely fitted in. I was the pantomime cow sent to a real dairy farm, the plastic flower in the bouquet, the laminate plank in the woodpile. What made it worse was looking on from the sidelines while everyone else just got on with school life. The flirting, the rugby, the classes — none of it came easily. Of course there were a couple of people who had it worse than me. One girl did look very like an aardvark, another permanently smelled of dried pee, and one poor boy was put in a wardrobe and pushed down a flight of stairs. I might have felt isolated and alone, but I knew that being ignored was better than any alternative I could hope for.

The school was set up to educate the children

of Protestants in the region. Due to the large catchment area, about half the pupils were boarders. As my father's job moved our family quite often, I spent about three years out of my total six in the boarding school. I know this will conjure up Enid Blyton stories or *Tom Brown's Schooldays*, but this was Ireland. The school was attached to a working farm — cattle walked past the classroom windows on their way to milking; the wind in the wrong direction could give Sports Day a very piggy feel; and every year the school held a disco called the Spud Hop to thank pupils for helping with the potato harvest.

From the road it looked imposing. It was a large white building perched on the brow of the hill with fields stretching out in front of it. As the number of pupils increased, various extensions were added on and a selection of temporary prefabs were erected to house classes. I don't know much about building standards but the fact that the foot of our religious affairs teacher went through the floor while he was drawing a map of the Holy Land on the blackboard would suggest they were not structures designed to last.

The girls' dormitories were in the main building but the boys slept in an old farmhouse in the grounds. Every night, after a mysterious dinner of grey meat and a couple of neon-bright hours doing prep (homework), we snaked our way down the pitch-dark avenue to bed. Insults and jokes would ring out in the giant stillness of the night, while the strange fashion for attaching steel tips to our shoes provided flurries of sparks to light up the darkness.

Nothing had been done to adapt the house to its new function, so bunk beds sat in rooms that were clearly meant to house sofas or large oak dining-room tables. I can remember a shack-like structure attached to the back of the building where we kept our tuck boxes full of stale biscuits. What I have no recollection of are any showers or bathrooms. As basic as it was, I assume we did have them but I can only guess that in the three years I spent as a boarder, I didn't wash that much.

A little like my relationship with the whole island, I can now look back and see that this manure-soaked, bare-boards education did have its benefits. The pupils might have been mainly from farming backgrounds but scattered amongst them were troubled city kids being given a second chance, plus the children of exotic foreigners who had been drawn to Ireland by the lure of unpasteurised milk and donkeys weighed down by baskets of turf harvested from the bog. In

retrospect, I realise what a privilege it was to be exposed to such a varied and strangely cosmopolitan group at an early age, as it set me up to be able to talk to anyone and only be intimidated by a very few, as I made my way into the big, bad world. The exam results back then suggested that we weren't getting the best of educations, but by not spoon-feeding us or putting us into some sort of educational hot-house, we learned to think for ourselves — when I got to university, the convent girls and Christian Brother boys really struggled when they were asked what *they* thought, rather than being told what they thought. I may not have received any As in my exams, but I did have opinions and that was thanks to my school on the farm.

When I was asked to be the guest of honour at the school's prize day a couple of years ago, I was both thrilled and apprehensive. Although I had managed to make some sort of success out of my life, it was due to a combination of tenacity and luck — I was hardly the poster child for education. I really struggled to think of what to say to the audience. I had no real stories about my time at the school and yet I felt that just saying I had spent my six years waiting to leave and trying to get out of playing any sports wasn't what they wanted either. In the end, I opted to speak to the boy I had been.

I had been one of the kids at the back of the hall who weren't being handed any of the glittering prizes. What did I wish someone had told me back then? Speaking to those young people turned out to be a real privilege and

50

oddly moving. I told them that they had more time than they thought. Time to make mistakes, time to start again. I told them they had choices and how important it was to keep as many as they could available to them. I remembered how defeated I had felt facing a huge wall of exams and how my life had seemed over before it had begun. I hadn't even bothered to dream of any kind of creative future because there had been no chance of it coming true.

I tried to explain to the scrubbed faces seated in front of me that no matter how good or bad their results, they would wake up tomorrow and life would go on. Young people thinking about their lives and careers have very fixed ideas of success but as we grow older, that changes. When I went to drama school we only dreamed of seeing our names up in lights. Twenty years later, at a reunion, some of us had achieved that but others had new careers, families, triumphs we could never have imagined. One woman had developed multiple sclerosis and for her, just getting to the reunion that day was her victory.

I don't know if I bored or illuminated the students that day, but I enjoyed talking to my teenage self and realising that fifty years on this planet had taught me something.

* * *

My university in Cork has been kind enough to give me an honorary doctorate. This was a particular surprise given that I dropped out of my degree after two years. Another honouree that day was the journalist and broadcaster, Fergal Keane. As I confessed to him my drop-out status, he revealed he hadn't even managed to get accepted. Another example of life not having to begin and end with exam results.

When I arrived at university in 1981, I loved it. Suddenly, here were people who read novels for pleasure, watched films with subtitles and strode purposefully across the campus in flapping, oversized trench coats. I had found my tribe: pretentious eighteen-year-olds!

The next two years were like a mighty pendulum. The first twelve months had me riding high, making friends, living in bedsits and enjoying my lectures; the next twelve found me brought low by depression and an overwhelming desire to leave.

I'm not sure how it all happened so fast but I suppose it was a combination of heartache and exam pressure. A summer spent in London had also made Cork seem very small and the only sort of love available to me seemed to be unrequited. There was no older me to explain that these feelings would pass by themselves and that there was no need to run away to America. Of course, in retrospect I'm glad I did, but back then one more year and a degree of some sort would have made my parents so very happy and proud — being a feckless university drop-out might have brought me joy but for them, it was just a whole heap of worry.

It was sad that my father was no longer around to see me in my finery processing through the Victorian cloisters into the book-lined Aula Maxima to get my scroll, but at least inviting the rest of my family to share in the bun-fight seemed like some sort of thank you, however tardy, for the amount of money that had been wasted on my aborted studies.

It was a very hot day and after sitting through the ceremony and listening to more Latin and Irish than I ever thought I would, there was a very welcome drink for everyone on the quadrangle outside. After mingling for a while and letting my mother revel in the glamour of the occasion, I asked my friend, John, who works at the college, what I should do with my ceremonial gown. He said I could keep it.

I guess my face must have betrayed something as I looked down at the cheap nylon material.

'Or,' he suggested, 'you could just leave it there,' and he pointed to a bench.

'Really?'

'Yes, go on.'

I walked over and draped the gown over the back of the bench. A man was standing next to it holding a glass of wine.

'Did you like it?' he asked.

'Sorry, like what?'

'The gown. I made them.'

What were the chances? I looked at the garment, now hanging there limply like abandoned swamp weed.

'Yes, it was lovely.' I thought about trying to explain: it was a hot day; I was flying without a bag . . . but I decided against it. I hope he just assumed I felt the gown was too beautiful to keep. I gathered my sister, brother-in-law and

53

mother, and we made our escape shortly after that.

★ ★ ★

Perhaps the most surprising honour Ireland has bestowed on me is having a river walkway in Bandon named after me. As it was the town in which I had spent most of my childhood and as the place where my family still live, the council decided it should mark my existence and links to the place in some way.

At first it was proposed they erect a statue of me. My mother showed me the letter and the accompanying look of horror on her face told me all that I needed to know about what she thought of the proposal. I wrote back to the council explaining that while I was very flattered, I'd prefer they didn't. Apart from how ugly the thing would look, I had visions of the vandalism and the sad day in the not-so-distant future when every passer-by would simply mutter: 'Who the fuck is that?' On top of these concerns was the expense to the town at a time when every euro counted.

The council did what councils do and had another meeting. It was decided that a new river walkway would bear my name. This seemed less fraught with difficulty, so I agreed and said I would come back to unveil the plaque.

As it happened, the 'plaque' turned out to be much bigger and more prominent than I had expected. It stands to one side of a bridge near a bus stop where in my youth I spent many hours waiting to be transported to the sophisticated urban wonders of Cork.

The day of the unveiling was grey and misty and I found myself like some dead-beat local politician making a speech from the back of a flat-bed truck holding a microphone that was designed to transform every speaker into Stephen Hawking. I spoke about roots and how the road out, which had been all I had been interested in, had also turned out to be the road home.

The formal proceedings over, the bunting was taken down and the walkway returned to being a place where people stroll. Perhaps as they step in dog shit or see an old pram bobbing along in the river, they will think of me. In addition, the sign itself has given my sister and mother a new interest in life: 'Still no graffiti on it,' they chirp, when I talk to them on the phone.

* * *

In the end, the strongest link one can have with anywhere is family. Blood ties are more binding than any other and after losing my father, it made what remained of our little clan seem all the more precious. Unusually for an Irish family, there is just me and my sister Paula. There is a slight sense of history repeating itself, however, since my father left just one sister, Aunt May, while my mother has just one brother, Uncle Ivan. It is not a family tree dripping with fruit.

Unlike me, my sister decided to stay and has lived her whole life in or near Bandon. So far her three children, all grown up now, have chosen to do the same. I'm not sure where my parents' vagabond tendencies came from, but I appear to have been the only one to inherit them.

My mother, undimmed by age, now lives in a sort of widows' row. It seems the men go first and the ladies are left to play bridge, keep their houses the way they want them and have nights out at the theatre. I see it as their reward for all the extraordinary sacrifices and hard work they endured with husbands and kids over the years. The other thing it means is that my mother is now free to travel. San Francisco, Venice, Paris, Seville, New York, Cape Town and, of course, London.

When my mother announces that she is coming to stay for the weekend I know exactly what is going to happen: 'I get in on the Thursday and I leave on the Wednesday . . . ' That, Mother dear, may *contain* a weekend, but it is in fact a week. But the feeling is that it's not worth getting on a plane for anything less.

My mother watches the chat show I make each week but she's not especially keen to sit in the audience. Her rationale is that she can see me whenever she wants and since the show is beamed into her living room, why leave the house? The requests for tickets only come for *Strictly Come Dancing* ('Hello dear,' said Sir Bruce to my mother as he walked by her seat at the edge of the dance floor. 'For God's sake,' she said to me, 'I'm younger than he is!') and the talent searches I hosted with Andrew Lloyd Webber.

In 2008, my mother came to see an episode of the search for Nancy in the show *I'd Do Anything*. It was to prove a longer and more dramatic trip than either of us could have guessed. On the Monday we were walking the dogs near where I live, along the river. I remember it was a warm day and we were heading towards St Katharine Docks to sit outside and have some lunch. One minute we were chatting and the next I turned to look at her and she'd disappeared — she'd fallen face-first onto the pavement that had tripped her. I bent down to pick her up.

'No,' she moaned, 'I've broken my wrists.'

At the time I didn't realise how common this is with older people who fall, and I assumed she was exaggerating. I rang my PA, Becky, who is also a trained paramedic — embarrassingly, opening my post and making restaurant reservations pays better than saving lives! She guided me through getting my mother to lie on her back while we waited for an ambulance. By then, a little group of concerned locals had gathered. Two gardeners from the nearby park held a sheet of plastic aloft as a makeshift shade from the sun and glasses of water were magically produced. Kindness will find you when you need it most.

The ambulance took my mother to the Royal London Hospital in Whitechapel. It was the nearest and, luckily, also where the victims of the worst road accidents are brought by air ambulance, so the trauma unit is exceptional.

There, they confirmed my mother's diagnosis — she had two broken wrists. She was operated on and titanium plates inserted. Better than new, she just needed to recuperate.

She was put in a small side ward but I was worried that because she couldn't even ring the bell or get herself a drink, she would be overlooked and get dehydrated or worse. I rang a doctor friend of mine and he recommended the best private hospital for bones. Throwing money at the problem, I arranged for her to be transferred to the leafy loveliness of north London and a very comfortable private room. I felt like a very good son.

Whenever I visited that week, I did notice that my mother seemed very weak and often sleepy. I assumed this was to do with the trauma of the fall and the fractures. I was wrong. The following Saturday I was at the BBC preparing for that night's live show of *I'd Do Anything* when my phone rang.

'Is this Mr Norton?'

'Yes.'

'This is Dr Blah-Blah from the hospital. Your mother's condition has deteriorated considerably. Are you able to come to see her?'

I felt the ground lurch beneath my feet. I had been there only a couple of hours earlier. How bad could she be?

'Are you saying that I *should* come and see her?' My heart was racing.

'I can't say that.'

'All right,' I said, swallowing hard, trying to stay calm. 'If she was your mother, would you come?'

'Yes, yes, I would.'

My world collapsed. I ran to find the producer of the show, Suzy Lamb. She came out of the control room. I wonder what she thought I was going to say? 'My mother — I have to . . . ' I couldn't continue.

Suzy and the rest of the team were great. Tissues were found and it was decided I shouldn't drive, so a taxi was ordered. A sudden thought: my sister Paula. Should I call her? Everyone agreed that I didn't have a choice — I must let her know.

The phone call nobody wants to make. Both crying, we agreed she would get the next flight and I'd see her at the hospital.

When I got there, the doctor brought me into his office. He tried his best to explain my mother's condition and how, somehow, some of her diabetes medication had caused an adverse reaction to other drugs that had been given. All I really heard was this final, awful sentence: 'If there is anything you'd like to say to your mother, now would be the time to say it.'

It was like a punch to the stomach. Why hadn't I understood before? Mum wasn't just very sick — she was going to die.

I crept into her room and the nurse left us alone. I said the only thing I wanted her to hear: 'You are going to live.'

It was explained to me that my mother needed an intensive care unit but that this hospital didn't have one, and none of the nearby NHS hospitals had beds available. I remember thinking, I bet the Royal London had an ICU. I'd been a fool. Almost hesitating, the doctor then revealed that the private hospital next door did have one, and beds were available.

Why were we even discussing this? 'Well, let's get her in there!'

The doctor paused, choosing his words. 'It is very expensive.'

I would sell my house. I didn't care. This was literally her lifeline.

In a grim glimpse into the future of healthcare, I crossed the road with my credit card while my mother followed behind on a gurney. I had never been happier to have money, and yet I knew this wasn't right — I felt like I was entering a place where people might come after being wounded in a gunfight at a casino, or where the foreign despot came to buy a new kidney.

The money paid, my pale husk of a mother was whisked through shiny doors into the hallowed halls of health.

Upstairs, a new doctor explained that I couldn't accompany my mother as she was going to have dialysis and tests. It would be a few hours, so I should go home.

After all the intense emotions of the last few hours I felt deflated. My mind snapped back to Television Centre. I checked my watch. I could make it, and it was something to do.

John Barrowman had rehearsed the show in case I didn't get back in time. Still, I wondered if he'd have to step in halfway through the programme: could I do this?

The team, the panel and the girls vying to be Nancy were all very sweet and supportive to me, and it turned out that I got through it without anyone noticing a thing. I'm not proud of being able to present a shiny-floored TV show while my mother was lying in an intensive care unit, but it was a welcome distraction. One of the panel, the great Barry Humphries, said it best. Just before we went on air he held my shoulders and told me, 'You are very lucky. You have been given a task.' I have no recollection of the programme that night but those talented girls and the musical lord got me through some very dark hours.

Back at the hospital, I arrived at the same time as my sister and together we crept towards my mother's bed. Her crystal-blue eyes were open and she smiled at us. A huge weight lifted from my shoulders. The light at the end of the tunnel was getting a lot brighter. We chatted for a while and then myself and Paula headed home.

Wine. Never has a glass been so welcome. We sat talking on my new couch. It had been going to be the one piece of furniture I kept nice, protected from the wear and tear of the dogs — within the next few minutes, Bailey and Madge were both snuggling up to us on it, aware that all was not right.

'Should these dogs be up here?' my sister asked.

Our mother was alive. 'It doesn't matter.' Because nothing else did.

★ ★ ★

My mother's troubles weren't quite over, though. I had no idea, but there is a condition called intensive care psychosis. It's caused by all the beeping machines and people coming and going, which means it is never possible to get deep sleep, and eventually patients can start to lose their mental faculties.

Of course Mum got it. At first it was quite funny: she thought her little dog Proby was in the bed, and she had been on several boat trips overnight and been invited to a wedding. At one point, one of the many specialists she saw was standing at the foot of the bed. The doctor was black.

My mother stared at him long and hard. 'If you're here . . . ' she paused, trying to get to grips with the mystery, 'then who's making my dinner?'

Paula and I laughed. It wasn't as if my mother had been raised on some cotton plantation with servants at her beck and call. The doctor did not laugh.

We stopped laughing too when the psychosis took a darker turn and she thought people were trying to hurt her. She was also remembering things from her childhood, real or imagined, which she found very upsetting. We asked the nurse if people always recovered from the condition our mother was suffering from. 'Usually,' came the unreassuring reply.

After being discharged from the hospital, Mum stayed with me for two months with hot and cold running nurses to look after her. For a woman who had been so fiercely self-reliant her whole life, she seemed to enjoy the novelty of 'help'. Perhaps she *had* been a child of the plantation.

When she was strong enough and my series

had ended, we headed back to Ireland. I had the perfect place for her to recuperate: my beautiful house in West Cork that I call home.

★ ★ ★

Every summer for two or three months, I run a sort of informal bed and breakfast at my house by the sea. This isn't a second income stream — I'm simply trying to convey to the reader the turnover of visitors and the amount of laundry and egg scrambling that goes on. Having my mother there was no extra trouble and I know she always enjoys it.

Given how strait-laced she appeared to be when we were growing up, she seems to have embraced modern Ireland with both arms. She is always the life and soul of the party and blossoms as she holds court for my friends. When she's on good form she'll head to bed at the end of the evening waving jazz hands and announcing, 'Goodnight, everybody!' as if she has just come to the end of her one-woman Vegas show. I had worried that after her fall and near-death experience she would never be independent again but happily she has bounced back. Obviously she still has the ability to drive me crazy — she is my mother, after all — but now after a particularly irritating run-in over something in the kitchen ('That gravy looks very runny') I can remind myself of how upset I was when I thought I had lost her. Life lessons.

When I first bought the house in Ireland and started inviting friends to stay, I was very keen and would arrive early at Cork airport, buy a posh coffee from the only Starbucks in Cork, which for some reason was situated beside the car-hire desks on the concourse (good news for haters of global corporate greed, it's now gone), and wait impatiently. I would then drive my visitors the hour and a half back to my lair by the sea, giving them the standard tour: my old school, our first house, I worked there on Saturdays . . . the usual sort of thing, until we reached the house. Nowadays I have an arrangement with a local man who drives guests for me. I'm told his tour is slightly different in that it is a litany of fatal car-crash sites, drownings, house fires and suicides, climaxing with the memorial for the 329 victims of the 1985 Air India disaster; though thanks to his very strong accent, one visitor thought they had heard about a freak Indian tornado that had killed many locals. An hour-and-a-half drive can seem very long indeed.

The house. I first saw it in 2003 on the sort of day when people take the pictures for postcards. I had been keeping an eye out for a bolthole by the sea in West Cork for quite a while. My vision had been of some fisherman's cottage with a couple of bedrooms by a small rocky cove with the smell of bread just out of the oven and a catch of fresh mackerel sizzling on the grill. It turns out such places don't exist or, if they do, I couldn't find them.

What my sister Paula did discover was a glossy brochure for an imposing, five-bedroomed house set in four acres of beautifully planted gardens with green lawns sweeping down to the ocean.

My mother was furious. The price tag! 'What does he want with that?' Against her better judgement, a viewing was arranged.

When my sister called the estate agent to set up a suitable time, they politely asked if she had seen the brochure. She said that she had.

'Well, it's nothing like that,' came the tart reassurance.

The estate agent wasn't wrong. The photographs of rooms filled with plump chintz sofas and gilt-framed oil paintings were in reality grim bare cells with pigeon droppings on the floors and strange fungal growths stuck to the walls. The manicured sweeping lawn was now just a lumpy meadow. Why would any owner let it get into this terrible state?

The one thing that remained intact was the view. My sister and I picked our way through the long grass towards the edge of the sea and an old pine tree that looked like a pregnant pensioner with its twisted branches and swollen trunk. At its base we found an ancient stone bench and we sat down. In front of us a cloudless blue sky and a panoramic view across Dunmanus Bay towards Mizen Head; to the left, the pier with a few trawlers tied up; and to the right a small cove edged by trees leaning into the winds of winters past. It was paradise. I turned to my sister and we both agreed that the exorbitant price of the house was worth it for that bench and the view alone.

Trying to buy the property turned out to be a very Irish story indeed. I put in an offer. It was rejected. Obviously I was disappointed but it was as much as the house was worth at the time and, I might add, a great deal more than it is worth now. A few months later I was on the phone to the same estate agent about another place I had seen advertised. They told me the original house was still available. 'Well,' I said, 'my offer is still available too.' Mysteriously, this time it was accepted.

An old school friend was acting as my solicitor and as she tried to do the deal, a strange story came to light. The house had been owned by a South African woman and I had assumed I was buying it from her. It turned out I wasn't. Some years previously, she had put the place up for auction and a British film star had been very interested. Neither he nor his West Cork solicitor had been able to attend the auction so the solicitor had sent her sister to bid on the star's behalf. He got it. The sister had signed whatever papers were needed and the deal was done.

I have since talked to the actor in question and he explained what happened next. His solicitor was very diligent and took months sorting out all the various complications over the deeds, rights of way and confusing boundaries. In that time, the actor simply got cold feet. He saw a time when he would end up in *EastEnders* just to pay for new roof tiles. His money had already been transferred to West Cork, but he phoned his solicitor and explained that he was going to pull out of the sale. In a very Irish way of doing business, she understood and returned his money.

My friend discovered the next part of the story. When the South African seller was told that the star had changed his mind, it transpired she didn't share the same 'Irish' way of doing business. She pointed out that the contract had, in fact, been signed by the solicitor's sister and the sale was going ahead. Conversation over. So it turned out that I was buying the house from someone who had never wanted to own it and, as a consequence, had hated the property and all it reminded him of. No wonder he had allowed it to sit and deteriorate!

All this might explain why the sale went through at the pace of a glacial snail. At one point we were waiting several days to hear from their office when we got a message saying that, due to unforeseen circumstances, the office had shut early that day. That afternoon, my friend sent me an email with a news story attached. A man had walked into their office and set himself alight. My friend added a PS: 'God forgive me, but I can understand the man's frustration.' I said the jokes could get dark.

It took a full year before my sale was complete and the keys were mine. Another year went by while the place was gutted inside and out and then finally there it was, returned to its former glory, my treasured gem by the sea.

★　★　★

When I go back for the summer I take the ferry with the dogs in the back of the car. With the various toilet breaks and pit stops for Scotch eggs, the journey takes around thirteen or fourteen hours, but as the car eases its way down the gravel drive and comes around the trees to find the view fully revealed it is absolutely worth it. The engine turned off, the dogs released and bounding with joy across the lawn, I am as close to perfectly happy as I think I ever will be.

I assume my friends love it almost as much as I do because I get a very high rate of repeat bookings. With a great selection of restaurants, swimming, kayaking, a well-stocked wine fridge and, of course, the late nights spent in the pub next door; these are our usual activities. People arrive full of plans to see historic sites and hike ancient trails, but the narcotic mood of relaxation soon overtakes them. How much nicer to watch a boat sail away across the diamond-strewn swell of the sea than to actually have to get on a boat and go sailing? One year, for no good reason, we tried pony trekking. It was not a great success. When we got to the stables it turned out that not one of us had any experience with horses, so each of us was given a young local girl to lead our steed. Five middle-aged gay men perched awkwardly on horses being led up the side of a mountain by children was closer to something from the end of the Roman Empire and further from the casual, sporty day out we had imagined.

Every year, a first-time visitor will suggest kayaking out to the island. This is a narrow strip of land about half a mile from shore, known locally as Owen's Island. We all assure them that we've done it and it is an inhospitable place full of nettles and seagull shit. For some reason, they always think we are trying to deny them the keys to paradise and they go anyway. An hour later they return, legs covered in angry red welts and clothes that carry the unmistakable stench of guano.

The local population is, I'm sure, slightly bemused to see me walking through the nearest town of Bantry on market day followed by my various bands of merry men, but not once has anyone ever been anything less than welcoming, friendly and helpful. I wish the same could be said of cosmopolitan London with all its sophistication and diversity. Homophobia has become a hot topic in Ireland. The problems of Northern Ireland led to the introduction of a law criminalising statements to incite hatred. Interestingly, the first use of the law was by a gay group outraged by comments made by a famous American singer from the stage at a Dublin concert. It may not have been what the legislation was designed to tackle but it made Ireland think. If you don't like being hated or discriminated against, then maybe don't do it to other people.

Growing up, I felt people couldn't connect the dots between the concept and the reality. People would happily rail against the sinful depravity of homosexuality while at the same time singing the praises of Brian and Kevin at number 17: 'Great neighbours. They keep their place immaculate and feed the cat when we go on holidays. Lovely lads.'

Small-town Ireland also makes a nonsense of celebrity. I was giving a talk to a local youth group and a girl asked me what it was like being famous. It was a very hard question to answer but, in a flash, it suddenly dawned on me: being famous was simply like living in Bantry — walking down the street, everyone knows who you are and when you are doing your shopping, there are always people you try to avoid. Afterwards, it struck me that my success on television was probably one of the reasons I found Ireland a more comfortable place to be. Growing up in a town where everyone knew your name and where your family lived I found claustrophobic and constricting — but now that happens to me walking down London's Oxford Street. No wonder I preferred being in the market square in Bantry, where at least I also saw many familiar faces and people I knew from local businesses or from chatting in the pub. Oddly, the smaller the place, the more 'being off the telly' becomes just another job and not a reason to stand out in the crowd.

★ ★ ★

Living in London, it's easy to forget that people can talk to each other. I walk my dogs around Wapping past hundreds of people on pavements and in parks and it is very rare a smile is exchanged or the silence broken. I occasionally get 'Are you Graham Norton?' 'Love the show' or a simple 'Faggot!' but for most people making their way through the capital, you soon learn that people generally only speak to you when they are (a) crazy, (b) want money, or (c) both. We quickly learn the rules and for the most part they work. In Ireland it is impossible to imagine not saying hello or commenting on the weather. When I first started going back home again, it would always take me a day or two to stop thinking everyone I met was trying to sell me something or explaining why they needed £2 to get the train.

I know this is true of rural communities the world over, but talking seems to be something we in Ireland are especially gifted at. There are nights in the pub when my friends look on in slack-jawed incomprehension as someone opens their mouth and a torrent of words tumble free. Usually they don't have anything to say. Their gate fell down. Who put it there. The man who fixed it. The general state of gates in the area. I will then remember an 'interesting' fact about my own gate. They will know the man who owned the forge where they made it. Are they a relation of the man who delivers the stuff? And so it goes. A seamless gush of phrases and banter as traditional as a sing-song or drink-driving. It is talking for the pure pleasure of it and not to communicate a single thing. It is the human equivalent of barking or birdsong.

Of course, it isn't just me that has changed. While I've become more comfortable in my own skin, Ireland too has grown in confidence. It seems to have realised that it can embrace the modern world without losing its identity or what makes it such a special place. In fact, by knowing more about the world, we have come to truly appreciate all the things we're good at: the story telling, the craftsmanship, the music, the easy warmth. We didn't know what treasures they were until we travelled to lands that didn't have them. The tiny minds that ruled the earth when I was growing up are fast becoming an extinct species and in their place are generations of young people who revel in their liberalness. For years we were kept in a dark, musty room unaware that, outside, things that gave you joy weren't automatically a sin. With the curtains drawn back and the windows opened, Ireland has become a truly wonderful place.

If someone had told me as I waited to board a plane to New York in 1983 that one day I would move heaven and earth to spend three months every year in the country I was desperate to flee, I would have told them that they were crazy. Of course it helps that I have money now and the house I was lucky enough to buy is in one of the most stunning settings in the world, but there is more to it than that. When I'm around Irish people I laugh more and find I relax in a different way. There is a shorthand between us that comes from having a shared history. No matter how long I live in Great Britain, I will never have that bond that comes from referring to the children's TV show *Wanderly Wagon* (Google it) or the night Dana won the Eurovision Song Contest. As a kid such things have no value but at fifty, you start to notice that sometimes those are the only things that matter.

There will be people who will be surprised to find me writing with such affection about the country of my birth; they see me as someone who fled and that in embracing all things British I have denied my roots. Oddly, the thing that incenses these people the most is when I am commentating on the Eurovision Song Contest and I refer to the UK entrant as 'we' and the Irish act as 'they'. My Twitter feed lights up with hate-filled comments where 'traitor' is about the mildest of the insults. It does seem surprising that these people can't figure out that I am doing a job and being paid by the British Broadcasting Corporation. If they are that fiercely patriotic then perhaps they should stop watching the BBC and enjoy Marty Whelan's Irish-centric commentary on RTÉ. It could also be said that if your concept of national identity is solely based on comments made during a contest that doesn't even have a very firm grasp on what Europe is, then I'm not sure you should be addressing the subject at all.

In reality, things are much more fluid and less cut and dried. When I get on the plane to go to Cork, I feel like I'm going home, but equally when I get ready to board the return flight to Heathrow I also feel that I am homeward-bound. I know I'm not British, but it is the place I live, work, pay taxes and vote. The UK has given me my life, my friends and my career. Of course I feel like I belong, but that doesn't stop me feeling Irish: embracing one thing doesn't automatically mean rejecting another. We can be a member of more than one tribe. The people who don't understand that are the bullies, the homophobes and the racists. As the Ireland of the past has taught us, small minds thrive in small worlds.

★ ★ ★

Back to the regatta in West Cork and I was hosting a table quiz. The committee had decided that the event would have a Hawaiian theme.

This seemed to be tempting the great gods of weather to punish the occasion but the night stayed unusually dry.

A marquee had been erected and decorated appropriately with coconuts and candles. Due to the demand for tickets, some extra tables had been put in the room above the pub next door to the tent. The start of the quiz was delayed while we waited for the electrician to fix the connection to a speaker in the upstairs room. When he was finished, I tested the sound system.

'Can you hear me?'

'Yes!' came the clear reply. It turned out we didn't really need the high-tech connection.

I had assumed the great hordes had come because of some big cash prize but it transpired the prizes were trophies made of cut glass. They did not look very impressive. I may have mentioned this. It's possible I mocked the name of the lady who donated them. The crowd may have hooted with derision when I revealed that they were perpetual prizes. Hideous, and you didn't even get to keep them! At that point the local priest helpfully pointed out that the same lady who had her name over all the trophies was, in fact, sitting at a table in front of me. She smiled and waved. I moved on swiftly.

The pub, in order to capitalise on the tropical theme, had set up a *tiki* bar in what was normally an unused shed — grass matting and a few sticks of bamboo worked wonders. The staff had spent countless hours that day hollowing out pineapples in which to serve cocktails. I had never seen so many pineapples in one place before, and certainly never in Ireland. I have no idea what the buckets of pulp were used for — jam, sorbet, upside-down cakes, cattle feed . . . there was a great deal of it going spare. Finally, around seven o'clock in the evening, it was decided to make the first cocktail and serve it up in its exotic hand-hewn cup. Syrups, booze, juice and ice were all shaken up. The beautifully dressed pineapple with tiny umbrella and twin colourful straws was placed on the counter. The mix was lovingly poured in and, after a moment's pause, the whole drink simply oozed through the skin to flow all over the bar top and floor. No one dared look at the hundreds of hollow pineapples or the staff with cramped, sticky hands. That night, delicious fruity cocktails were served to all in smart plastic cups stuffed into pineapple shells. Problem solved.

The quiz questions ranged from international news to who had won Person of the Year on Sheep's Head (the correct answer was Peter the Meter, the man who travels the headland reading all the electricity meters). The winning table consisted of a young family and a couple of their children's friends. People cheered them but nobody took the outcome very seriously — the night was about seeing neighbours and friends while having a drink and some laughs. This was a modern Irish gathering but, in another way, it was as old as the stone walls surrounding the fields outside. Should a flat-capped ghost from days of yore have stumbled into the marquee that night, they might have been surprised to find an openly gay host or more pineapples than you'd find in the music video for 'Agadoo', but they would still have felt at home in an atmosphere that remains familiar to every Irish person. Amateur, ambitious, raucous and good-humoured. Ireland, you have come a long way and I am proud to call you home.

3

New York

Late one night in the early summer of 1983 I found myself on a bus with about forty other Irish students. Our flight from Dublin had been delayed and, of course, our levels of excitement meant any sleep on the plane had been out of the question. By now we were almost delirious. Our faces were pressed against the windows and we gasped at the size of the cars and the width of the highway. Billboards advertising films and shops we had never heard of lit up the black night that surrounded us as we hurtled towards New York from JFK. I think back to all the sweet, undisguised excitement and hope on that bus. Where are those young people now? What happened to their sense of adventure and wonder? At fifty, will it ever be possible to feel like that again?

The bus went into a tunnel and we all went quiet, our pale faces reflected in the windows. Every time I visit New York now I come through that same tunnel but coming out the other side has never again had the same theatrical dazzle. That night, it was as if someone had suddenly ripped back a curtain to reveal an enchanted kingdom — all at once lights filled the night and towered up into the sky. The cars were yellow.

The people black and white. Our driver growled into his microphone, 'Welcome to the Big Apple!' We cheered and squealed with delight.

Thirty years later, as I walk down 36th Street towards my house, the Chrysler Building on my left, the Empire State to the right, I am cheering still.

To be honest, after the initial excitement on my first visit, the whole thing just proved too much for me. We had all travelled together as part of a J1 visa scheme, which meant that Irish students could work in the States for three months. I had already decided that I was going to stay for longer — I just hadn't told anyone, particularly my parents, who were happily expecting me to return in September and finish my degree.

There was only one person I knew in the group, a girl called Louise who was studying at the art college in Cork. We didn't know each other well but clung to one another in this overwhelming urban unknown.

Everyone was staying in a YMCA on 23rd Street (which is now luxury condos). That first night, like the well-brought-up Irish children we were, everyone just walked around the block, stared up at the buildings, saw a homeless man shouting at a trash can, got frightened and went to bed.

You might have thought the clear bright morning would have made the city a little less intimidating and perhaps you'd have been right, if it hadn't been for our orientation class. For this, we were all piled into a room crammed with small desks, where a nice man welcomed us to the greatest city in the world. And then, in great detail, proceeded to explain all the ways we could get killed. Actually, I still follow some of his advice: walk by the kerb not the buildings, never look up, and if you have to check a map do it in a store or hotel lobby.

After the class we stepped tentatively out onto the sidewalk, every passer-by a potential killer. As far as I remember, all I did that day was a tour of the Rockefeller Center because I wanted to see the inside of the Radio City Music Hall. When the slick New York lady who was our guide told me she liked my outfit — jodhpurs and some sort of string vest — I felt I had the seal of approval from the whole city.

Looking back, I'm not quite sure why I got on a bus and left that afternoon. I think I was in a hurry to start my never-to-be-completed trip to Los Angeles in order to meet up with my pen-pal, the exotically named David Villapando. Our intense friendship remains in the form of long emotional letters, but all my attempts to track him down more recently have been fruitless. The other reason for a quick getaway was my realisation that the longer I stayed in New York the faster my £200 spending money would disappear. Younger readers may be thinking to themselves that, thirty years ago, £200 must have been a great deal of money. It wasn't. I was an idiot and it is a miracle I survived. It's for this reason that age and experience are the natural enemies of adventure.

That night and day in the Big grimy Apple was

to be the last I saw of New York for more than a decade. After a year in California, I returned to Europe and drama school in London. Trips to New York didn't appear to be on top of my list of things to do — 'Pay the phone bill' seemed to be the most I could wish for. Happily, fate would come to call and get me back to the great city, and for free.

★ ★ ★

Once I realised that my acting career wasn't going to follow the trajectory of Kenneth Branagh's or, in fact, that of any actor who actually had a job, I started finding new ways of showing off. Comedy monologues and skits took me to the Edinburgh Festival, where Emma Freud introduced me to the good people at BBC Radio 4.

Loose Ends, which, at the time of writing, is still going strong, presented with great aplomb by Clive Anderson, was back then a mix of comedy old and new. The great Ned Sherrin was the host. He had seen it all and yet despite that or possibly because of it, he always had a wonderful twinkle in his eye. He lived life with glee and collected moments like some people pick up shiny shells along the seashore. As one of the young comics on the show, I loved to sit in the pub after the broadcast and hear him tell his stories. Often I didn't know the long-gone luminaries he was talking about but I recognised the privilege of listening to one of the last great anecdotalists. Somebody once told me they overheard a conversation during the interval of

Ned's one-man show:

'The second half is completely different.'

'Oh — is it about living heterosexuals?'

Sadly Ned is now part of his own show — an old-school theatrical character who has passed away. His funeral was one of the most beautiful I have ever been to, with everyone smiling and crying as his coffin was carried out, his battered leather Gladstone bag perched on top, while the organist bashed out the theme tune to *The Archers*. It was pure Ned.

Part of my job on the show was to present reports on quirky and interesting events. Things like the Toilet of the Year awards or a rapping rabbi were the sorts of subjects I tackled. It is therefore astonishing that someone agreed to let me take a tape recorder to New York in order to capture the comedian and actor, Brian Conley, soaking up the sights and sounds of old Broadway as he prepared to take on the role of Al Jolson, in a new musical version of his life story.

I knew the PR of the show, Joy Sapieka, and her assistant, Ben Webster, from hanging around in late-night bars in Edinburgh. At the age of thirty-two, for the first time in my life, I appeared to be well connected, and I was to be flown out to New York in business class! My hotel room was paid for and, best of all, I had practically no work to do.

I had not been on many planes at this point in my life and had certainly never been invited to turn left by the air stewardess. Myself, Joy, Brian and his lovely wife, Anne-Marie, settled into our large, armchair-style seats. Joy's assistant, Ben, was travelling in economy. I promised to visit him during the flight.

Given that I had always travelled in the back of the plane, it was amazing how quickly the world of free champagne and leg room became like home. We had only been in the air for about half an hour when I decided to see how Ben was getting on. I pulled back the curtain that divided the two cabins and I remember I actually gasped. Compared to the serene world of sleep suits and linen napkins I had left, this looked like a documentary about refugees in a third-world country. I waved and smiled at a grim-faced Ben and headed back to where I so obviously belonged.

By then I had been living in London for quite a few years so I was surprised to find that the city of New York was still so intimidating. Maybe it was because I had watched too many episodes of Edward Woodward in *The Equalizer*, or perhaps I was still feeling the effects of that orientation class ten years before, but heading out by myself took all my courage.

I only knew one person in New York apart from my travelling companions. His name was Blaise Hancock and I had met him at the Daisy Chain, a club night at the Fridge in Brixton. We had only spent one evening together but thanks to Blaise's persistent letter-writing we had stayed in touch. In a world before mobile phones, I called his number and left a message on his answering machine, then I sat on my bed in the Marriott Marquis hotel in Times Square and looked out at the glittering, triumphant skyline that I knew from countless movies.

This was life, and I was not going to sit alone in my room, old chum.

I headed downstairs to get into a taxi. The only address I knew was Christopher Street. It was where the Stonewall riots had happened which signalled the birth of the modern gay rights movement. I would go and drink with my tribe and the city would seem less alien. With as much confidence as I could muster I announced to the driver, 'Christopher Street, please!' Easy. 'Which end?' came his reply.

Shit. I had not been expecting this complication. 'The busy end.'

I waited. The silent driver took off. Apparently my instructions had made sense and I was very pleased with myself.

About ten minutes later the driver pulled up and I paid him with a flustered wad of notes, so fearful of under-tipping that I probably gave him the fare twice over.

As he drove off, I looked around me. If this was the busy end of Christopher Street, I could only imagine the other end was a farm. The street was deserted. I walked slowly, looking for lone gunmen in every shadow. After about a block I saw a neon sign and a tired rainbow flag hanging exhausted above the door. My people! I walked in and looked around. A long wooden bar filled most of the space. TV screens dotted around the room were showing a mixture of music videos and soft porn. I don't think I was the only customer but it was fair to say that I had failed to find the heart of one of the world's most vibrant gay scenes.

I could have turned around and gone back to the hotel, but the thought of being bored in a bar seemed much more appealing than being mugged and murdered outside. I sat and nursed a beer. The famously friendly New Yorkers ignored me.

Eventually, two youngish guys stumbled in and sat on stools beside me. They were drunk. We got chatting. I spoke to one of them more than the other. I didn't find him that attractive but I figured that if I went home with him I was less likely to be gunned down in the street. His friend left us alone and it was decided we would head back to the hotel.

In the morning my temporary companion headed off to work, leaving me his number. It had been a fun distraction on my first night, but I already knew I wasn't going to call him. With a winning combination of jet lag and a hangover, I headed downstairs to start work.

Our day was spent wandering around theatres where Jolson had performed, and visiting the Algonquin Hotel made famous by Dorothy Parker. The most entertaining bits were the hours we spent in the back of stretch limos going from one location to the next, with Brian Conley keeping us all laughing with gossip and stories from a world I longed to be a part of.

Now, please be warned that the remainder of this story is quite complicated, so pay close attention!

Back in my hotel room I tried calling Blaise again and left another message. The TV had hundreds of channels compared to the UK's four and I used them to distract me from the fact I was in New York and appeared to have nothing to do.

The phone rang. Hurrah, Blaise to the rescue.

'Hi. How are you?'

'Good,' he giggled. 'What are you up to tonight?'

'Well, I was hoping to see you,' I replied.

He gave me the address of a bar and a time to meet.

I felt like a native New Yorker when I found the spot and walked in bang on time. Blaise wasn't there yet so I just ordered myself a drink and waited. This place was much busier than last night's haunt and every time the door opened I glanced over to see if it was Blaise.

Ten minutes had probably passed when I looked up and there was proof that the Apple wasn't that big: walking into the bar was the guy from the night before.

My heart sank, but I hoped that maybe he hadn't spotted me. Dashing that hope, he walked straight over. Almost as quickly as he said hello I blurted out that I was meeting a friend. I didn't want him to think that I was following him around the city. He tried to make a bit of conversation but I was as monosyllabic as possible. Eventually, worn down by my cold welcome, he started to chat to other people.

Being stood up is never a good thing but when it happens in front of the man you picked up the night before, it is especially humiliating. I gave Blaise a few more minutes and left. Back at the hotel, I expected to see the message light flashing on the phone but there was nothing.

The next morning before I headed out for

another day with my tape recorder, the phone rang. It was Blaise.

'What happened to you last night?' I asked.

'Sorry, what do you mean?'

I reminded him of our plan to meet. He knew of no such plan. In fact, he had been out of town for a few days and had only just picked up my messages. We chatted for a few more minutes but my head was swimming with what had happened. When I put down the receiver, the full horror dawned on me. I had never spoken to Blaise. The voice on the phone had, in fact, belonged to my new friend from the first night. He hadn't just happened to walk into that bar — I had arranged to meet him!

I stood in my room blushing when I remembered how I'd behaved. He must have thought his fun new pal from London was mentally unhinged. Since I had thrown away his number there was no possibility of explanation or apology. I had been stood up when, in fact, my suitor had been by my side. It was a dating first.

★ ★ ★

More years passed but then, as my career back in London eventually started to take off, the novelty of having money in the bank meant I was able to visit my urban crush more often. I started to get to know New York better and have favourite bars and neighbourhoods. Once the chat show *So Graham Norton* started on Channel 4 and BBC America began showing it in the States, I was even recognised a couple of times. New York began to feel like a home from home.

I made a series there for Radio 4 where I interviewed famous New Yorkers like Patricia Field, the stylist from *Sex and the City*; and Barbara Corcoran, the most successful estate agent in Manhattan. There was a small audience and we taped one show a night for a week. It felt great to pretend to live and work in this fabulous city.

Two days after we left, the twin towers came down. Our series was going to be called *Graham Norton's Big Apple Crumble*. It was never aired.

In November, just two months after the attacks, I was back for the International Emmys. The city felt different. The rest of America thinks New Yorkers are brusque and rude but compared to what we are used to in Britain, I have always found them incredibly welcoming and friendly. Now there was something else in their manner — they were grateful. No matter how uber hip and cool the store or restaurant might have been, the people who worked in them had the air of a dog that had been kicked. It was as if the most beautiful girl in school had been dumped by the biggest geek in the class. This confident, wonderful city was reeling with incomprehension that someone had slapped it so hard. What had it done to deserve this?

Channel 4 had flown myself and the producers of my chat show over, along with fellow nominees Simon Pegg and Jessica Stevenson (then Hynes), the stars of the sitcom *Spaced*. Oddly the International Emmys had put our shows in the same category, but there was no time for any real rivalry. There were dinners and receptions to attend and, once more — even under a thick layer of dust — New York dazzled us all.

On the night of the award show Jennifer Saunders and Joanna Lumley, still on the huge high of *Absolutely Fabulous*, walked on stage to rapturous applause. The nominations were read out and then the winner. We'd done it! I stumbled onto the stage, kissed Jennifer and Joanna, forgot to thank people and then proceeded to get very drunk in a series of clubs that began with velvet ropes and chandeliers and ended up with sawdust on the floor. It was perfect.

The next day, in a rush to get back to London to tape another chat show, I stood at the check-in counter for Concorde. Nowadays I meet people who are so frustrated that they will never get to experience the supersonic, pointed-nose thrill of that plane. Having done it a few times, I can reassure you that it was about as exciting as the shuttle from Heathrow to Glasgow, with cramped seats and the same little fold-down tray. In fairness, the tiny plate of food was lobster and caviar but after a couple of hours, that does little to cheer your stiff knees.

The passengers on Concorde, however, were as elite as you might imagine. The first time I took it, a suited steward was making his way down the aisle. 'Would sir/madam care for a glass of champagne after take-off?'

In my mind the correct response, given the price of the ticket was, 'Yes, please! A bucket of it!'

The lady seated behind me responded to the question with one of her own: 'Are you still serving the Taittinger '88?'

The steward purred with pride. 'Yes, madam, we are.'

'Then, no, thank you.'

It is possible to be too rich.

Given what had happened that September, even on Concorde the security was extremely strict. I only had a carry-on bag but I was attempting to transport an Emmy award — in the wrong hands, the sharp wings could have done a great deal of damage. I asked the nice woman behind the counter if I could bring it into the cabin. She looked doubtful. I was surprised Concorde didn't have a policy for award winners. She decided the only person who could give me permission was the captain. Happily, he didn't turn out to be the teeth-sucking jobsworth I had been expecting. He congratulated me on my win and waved me and my lethal weapon aboard.

That night, back in London, I lay slumped on my sofa with my shiny award on the coffee table in front of me. There was a documentary about

Hollywood playing on the TV and out of the corner of my eye, I spied a shot of a young Lucille Ball sitting at a table. In front of her was a shiny award, exactly the same as mine. I didn't whoop or punch the air, but I can't deny I did feel a definite warm glow. I had become a member of a very cool club.

* * *

I think I somehow became over-excited about my relationship with America and New York. A warm welcome is one thing, an award is always nice, but did I really need to buy a house there?

In 2002 we began producing *V Graham Norton*. The show was fairly similar to *So Graham Norton*, my chat show that had been running once a week for the past four years, but this one went out five nights a week. It was very ambitious and I remain really proud of the achievement, but from a personal point of view it was like joining the priesthood.

My commitment to the show was absolute but once we had proved we could make it, the gloss started to wear a little thin. Of course there were highlights. Being part of Channel 4 at that time was exciting: *Big Brother* was a huge hit and my show played off it, reaching audiences as large as the ones we now get on BBC One. I remember sitting on the terrace of the Oxo Tower restaurant one night; London was doing its best impression of New York, with lights reflecting in the wide expanse of the Thames. As I and the producers clinked glasses to another show done, I remember feeling at the heart of something for the first time. If this was what mainstream felt like, I was enjoying it. And that was probably when I began to seriously consider the offers that were coming in from the BBC.

The other change that five nights a week brought about was money — lots of money. I was working five times as hard and co-owned the production company, So Television, so the cash was rolling in, but I had no time to spend it.

Obviously I enjoy the trappings of wealth but equally I am my mother's son. There are things I refuse to spend money on (I still do my own laundry) and there is always a part of me that is mentally preparing for it all to end. More often than I care to admit I will make a little tally of what I'd be worth if I sold everything and how long it would last me; I may not be putting it in my trolley today, but I'm very happy to see there are bottles of wine for under a fiver. What goes up must come down.

Mysteriously, with a fatter bank balance comes a different class of post. Just like the day after my fiftieth birthday when a brochure from Saga Holidays landed on my mat, so with bigger pay cheques came posh magazines and brochures from luxury auction houses.

Over breakfast one morning, I was idly flicking through a catalogue that had come through the letterbox, when I spotted a photograph of a house in the property section. It was a mews house in New York and I fell in love with it.

I wasn't stupid enough to think I would actually buy it, but I liked looking at it. It was property porn and, as with porn, I knew the object of my desire would never be mine. The picture ended up on my desk at work. It wasn't in a frame or anything, but just lay on top of a pile of old scripts to help me dream during especially dull meetings. I showed it to my producer, Jon, and he surprised me by urging me to buy it: 'If I had your money, that is exactly what I would do.'

I began to think about it. Property in Manhattan was surely a good investment and it seemed like a very low-profile way of being wildly flash with my cash. Living in some leafy mansion in an under-populated bit of London didn't appeal, but this irrational indulgence was wildly tempting. I decided to go and see it.

Arriving in New York just to view a property is a very eye-opening experience — the real-estate sharks were in full swing. Word was out that an idiot with money was in town. I now had dozens of properties to see and a town car at my disposal. It was an amazing weekend where I saw some spectacular apartments and lofts, but there was only one that had stolen my heart — and it would steal a huge chunk of my wallet. I adored its setting in a little mews, its old-fashioned front door, the leafy roof terrace with its view of the Chrysler Building. On the down side, it was in the deeply unfashionable area of Murray Hill, but all I knew was that it was about six blocks from the Empire State Building and three from the tunnel that had delivered me to the city all those years before.

The house had been owned by the illusionist, David Copperfield, but I was buying it from Claudia Schiffer after she got it in some sort of separation settlement. I never met her during the negotiations but a few years later, I spotted her across the dance floor at the incredibly star-studded wedding reception for Sir Elton John and David Furnish. With the aid of booze-induced bravery, I went up to her and explained that I was the person who had purchased her old house. She looked at me as if I had asked her if she'd like to smell one of my farts and walked away. I presume she feels I should have paid more, or maybe someone told her that I had given away various beauty products she had left in the bathroom as prizes when I was doing a stand-up show in New York, culminating with her lady shaver. In the right hands, that could probably be used to clone her.

★ ★ ★

I'm not sure if it was simply because I was now a home-owner in the city, but for some reason I found myself working more and more in New York. On the strength of a certain notoriety gained from the show being aired on BBC America, some producers started bringing me to Manhattan to do stand-up shows. Back in Britain, I had done a short comedy tour but the venues had been so big it had been hard to have fun with the crowd, plus the travelling from one town to the next was boring and time-consuming. Doing a two- or three-week run in a small off-Broadway theatre suited me perfectly, however, and I loved the American audiences who came willing you to be funny.

The only night this failed to happen was when *Vanity Fair* decided to throw a party in my honour after one of the shows. Of course I was thrilled and flattered but there was a price to pay — the audience that night was full of people who worked at the magazine and their grey-skinned advertisers. For ninety minutes they sat and stared at me. I felt I could have been doing a Beckett monologue or pulling live trout out of my ass and they would have had the same vacant expressions.

As part of the show I had been doing in the UK I phoned people who had left personal ads in various gay magazines. It was fairly edgy at the time, and straight audiences had liked how naughty the whole thing seemed. In New York the personal ads were different and you couldn't get through to a real person. I was stuck for something to fill the time and I had already put the producers to the extra expense of providing a phone line and the equipment to patch the call through to the speakers. One night I was having a drink in a mid-town gay bar called Stella's. Although I had noticed the clientele was an odd combination of older gentlemen and younger Latino guys and there seemed to be an abundance of ATMs inside the venue, I didn't put two and two together until one of the cuter customers came over to talk to me. It was a hustler bar (of course it was) and the man speaking to me, called Sammy, did exactly that for a living. He was very funny and told me some great stories, especially one about a punter who had taken him back to his hotel. Once inside the room Sammy had noticed a miniature white picket fence squaring off a piece of the floor. Within it was a live chicken. Not just any chicken, the man explained — this was a showbiz chicken and had appeared in one of the *Babe* films no less. The man wanted Sammy to give him a blow job, but while the chicken was looking. Given that the bird had had no interest in seeing Sammy devour a fat worm, there was a great deal of shuffling about on his knees trying to remain in the chicken's eye line. It turned out that the punter was a showbiz agent and the bird was his most successful client. I suspect he took more than 10 per cent in commission.

After that, every night during my show I would phone Sammy and he would tell his chicken story or something equally outlandish. About twice a week I'd see him and give him some cash for his trouble. Given his tales from the world of hustling, I have no doubt this was the easiest money he had ever made.

On the *Vanity Fair* evening, it was the one part of the show that seemed to pique their interest perhaps because it wasn't me speaking.

The party afterwards was at the then brand-new W Hotel just off Times Square. As grim as the show had been I will admit it felt pretty glamorous to be attending a party thrown for me by one of my favourite magazines. Women who hadn't eaten since 1995 tried to make small talk with me but it soon ran out. Then: 'Where's Sammy, I wonder?' they giggled.

'Oh, he's right here,' I took delight in revealing, and led them over to the shaven-headed man wearing a leather waistcoat over a tanned bare chest.

When worlds collide. I loved it. These people might all have shared the small island of Manhattan, but they lived on different planets.

★ ★ ★

Channel 4, who seemed to have more money than sense, agreed to let us come to New York to do a week of shows of *V Graham Norton*. It coincided with my fortieth birthday and, on top of that, NBC had asked us to make a pilot episode of the chat show for them.

It was as exciting as show business could get.

Putting the shows together for the UK was a dream — great guests, enthusiastic audiences and wildly ambitious stunts and pranks filmed on the streets of the city.

The pilot for NBC was going less well.

American television executives are a different breed and travel in packs. As far as I can make out this is so that if something is a great success they can all take the credit and if it's a disaster, it's nobody's fault. Having been very excited about working with me, I now felt the suits we were dealing with were very much getting ready to try to avoid blame.

They had given us a list of acceptable guests and we had been pleased to see that a friend of the show, former Blondie singer Debbie Harry, was on it. We booked her. Two days before the taping of the pilot it transpired that while we had read their list of prospective guests, they hadn't — Ms Harry was not acceptable. Get someone else! In addition to this, they were being very difficult over the format rights and production deal.

Having had a great week, and on the eve of my fortieth birthday, I decided this NBC show was going to make me very unhappy. In a fit of diva drama I didn't know I had in me, I pulled the plug.

My poor agent, Melanie, and my business partner, Graham Stuart, sat in a small room with the network frenemies. My position was explained, but because of the sort of duplicitous creatures they were, they assumed it was some kind of bargaining tool — Debbie Harry was now a great guest and we would own all of the format and make the show ourselves.

No. Still no. Seriously no.

They finally accepted that it wasn't going to happen and sloped off into the evening happy about one thing only. They knew who to blame. Me.

Our production company did have to suck up quite a few of the costs, so not going to work that day ended up being a very expensive birthday present to myself.

With no NBC to bother us, we had a combination wrap-and-birthday party on the roof terrace of a bar and restaurant called The Park. I sometimes went to a Sunday night gay party up there where the hot tub ended up looking like a very unappetising bowl of boy soup, but I doubted my party would end up like that. Happily my friend Carrie Fisher was in town from LA and stopped by to say hello. She quickly worked out that it was, in fact, my birthday and was appalled she had nothing to give me. One of her minions ran back to their car and returned holding a large, heavy, star-shaped glass trophy from Tiffany that Carrie had just been given by the BiPolar Association of America. She insisted I take it and I have it still, beautifully engraved and perched on my mantelpiece in New York, a puzzle to anyone who rents my house.

Turning forty isn't that dramatic but, like any landmark birthday, it forces you to take stock. I knew I didn't want to continue doing five nights a week but going back to just one show on Channel 4 did seem like a retrograde step.

I began talking to the BBC. The idea was that So Television would get to pilot some big Saturday-night shows for me and, well, other stuff. It was pleasingly vague and also seemed very far off. In the meantime we would finish our contract at Channel 4 by doing a season of weekly shows from Manhattan called NY

Graham Norton. It was like their leaving gift to me. After that we were going to make our first ever series for an American channel.

In the wake of the disaster with NBC we met other broadcasters and decided Comedy Central was the best fit for us. The world was my oyster and New York was the pearl. Although I was essentially wandering into the unknown on both continents, I felt excited and fearless. I was the forty-year-old fool.

★ ★ ★

I truly do believe that part of my blind faith in the future stemmed from living in New York. The show was getting a lot of pre-publicity so we were perceived as 'hot'. I have no idea how they do it, but the guys holding the velvet ropes outside the cool clubs and restaurants suddenly seemed to know who I was. Encouraged by our American producers, I signed up a publicist and started being offered features in magazines and spots on the late-night talk shows. I felt like I was going to a Halloween party and my costume was an American celebrity. Of course I knew none of it was real, since cab drivers or people in the street didn't know me from Adam.

As well as working, I was using the Big Apple as an even bigger playground. I might have been forty but I refused to go quietly. Every night of the week I knew where the party was and more often than not I was there. By this stage I had acquired a small group of really good friends in the city who knew all the inside scoop. Not worried about tabloid attention or kiss-and-tell merchants, I made up for what I felt was lost time. I hadn't exactly been living under a rock in London but this was full on. I look back now on all the parties and boys and wonder how I survived. I had assumed that 'the city that never sleeps' was just an expression but it turned out that it was true, and it was killing me.

In the middle of all the party carnage I met Kristian, who was to become Bailey the labradoodle's bad daddy. I still adore him and whenever I'm in New York we always seek each other out, but back then it was all too much. Ignoring every shred of common sense we possessed, a turbulent romance went on for nearly five years. He was too young; I was too old. I wanted a relationship; he wanted another drink. In the middle of one of our many fights I remember screaming at him, 'I gave you my heart and you left it in the back of a cab.' That sort of sums it up. I know he cared for me at the time but I was ready to leave the party to be with him while he had so much more living to do. We broke up and got back together more times than I care to remember.

Every time I found myself single I was never too heartbroken to go out, though. The actor, the go-go dancer, the interior decorator, the air steward — I made my way through the book of clichéd jobs for gay men. Now, when I walk around my house in New York, I see so many ghosts and hear half-remembered drunken conversations. It was a last, over-enthusiastic farewell to whatever youth I had left. I still drink and party, but

100

it's not quite the same as that hedonistic year in the city that has no interest in bedtime.

★ ★ ★

The promise of success in the States is so overwhelming it takes precedence over everything else. Somewhere in the back of my mind I guess I imagined that the American version of the show would take off and I would never have to go back to work in Britain. Given how content I am with my life now, I can't believe I ever felt like that but I know it's true. A lot has changed in ten years.

At some point, while we were still taping the Channel 4 show for the US, my mother decided she was going to come and visit. She had last been in the city fifty years earlier when she had been working as a secretary in Toronto and she and some of her friends had driven through snow storms in a borrowed car to see the greatest city on earth. I remember as a young boy staring at a creased black and white photograph of her clear, smiling face standing on the observation deck of the Empire State Building. Half a century later, she was back.

I've never been able to reconcile the woman who is my mother with the girl who bought a berth on a freight ship and sailed all the way to Canada from Belfast. Once she arrived, she rented a room in a boarding house run by a woman who stank of rum, got herself a job and stayed in Toronto for a year before heading home. Now, the idea of a gap year may be

101

commonplace, but for the young woman living with her parents and brother in a terraced house in post-war Northern Ireland it was as unlikely a trip as canoeing down the Amazon with nothing but a letter opener to protect you. How had that person become the woman who ironed pillow cases and tea towels?

Because I had to work, I knew I wouldn't be able to babysit my mum all the time. As I didn't want to risk her being a grey-haired version of Macaulay Culkin in *Home Alone 2: Lost in New York*, I bought her a pay-as-you-go phone so that she could call me if she needed anything.

I don't know what she was thinking, but when I suggested she take the phone, it was as if I had asked my mother to carry a homemade bomb in her handbag. She flatly refused it.

On her first day, when it was time for me to go to the office, she decided she wanted to explore the city on one of those hop-on/hop-off bus tours. That seemed safe enough so I took her to the ticket office and waved her off. I would see her later back at the house.

When I got home there was no sign of my mother. And, of course, no way to contact her. Trying not to worry I sat and waited. At least two hours went by and I was standing on the street keeping an eye out for her, wondering when I could reasonably call the police, when I caught sight of her familiar blue coat and grey hair making their way down the hill towards my gate.

My delight and fury would be a good preparation for dog ownership. It turned out she had got off the bus on the west side of

Manhattan somewhere around 50th Street and walked home. Why? At first she tried to tell me that she hadn't seen any cabs but because that was so patently untrue she eventually confessed that she had, in fact, left the house without my address or phone number. So she hadn't hailed a taxi because she had no idea where to tell the driver to take her. Her arrival at my doorstep might have been physically and mentally impressive, but it was mostly luck.

Later that night, just to make matters more difficult, the city was visited by a very unseasonal snow storm. The next morning the pavements were thick with snow and slippy. These were not ideal conditions for an Irish pensioner to explore New York by herself, so I organised a driver and a car to be at her disposal all day and again waved her on her way. My mother was going to the Metropolitan Museum of Art.

When I got out of my meetings around lunchtime I called the driver to make sure everything was OK and find out where they were. The driver revealed sheepishly that my mother had sent him away. Apparently she had taken him to the museum but then told him that she didn't need him for the rest of the day.

This time it was fury without any of the delight, but at least when I got home she was there. She could offer no explanations. It was like the mobile phone — she was so determined not to be any bother to me that she couldn't see how extremely bothered I was.

In between wanting to kill her, I took her sight-seeing. We sailed a boat around the island,

103

watched Broadway shows and ate in fancy restaurants, but there was only one thing she really wanted to do. My mother wanted to get back to the top of the Empire State Building. I pointed out the snow-filled clouds — the visibility would be awful — but she didn't care. Fifty years had passed and she would wait no longer.

High on the 102nd floor, wrapped up against a winter wind, my mother happily posed for photographs.

In her house in Bandon she now has her two photographs taken half a century apart, sitting side by side. The hair colour may have changed and the face has some extra lines but the smile remains the same, while her pale blue eyes full of wonder stare out at the city in both frames. The biggest surprise is to see that behind her, despite the years that have passed, the skyline remains remarkably unchanged. The twin towers have come and gone but somehow these twin photographs tell you that the glory and excitement of New York will go on for ever.

* ★ ★

The first slight hiccup at Comedy Central was that all the executives who had been really keen to sign me up left. 'Not to worry,' I thought. 'I'm sure the new guy will be just as keen.'

It turned out he wasn't that new. His name was Doug Herzog and this was his return to Comedy Central — he had left as head of the channel a few years before to work for one of the networks, but was now coming back. Strange.

I got an invitation from his office to go for lunch. I bought a bright jacket, trimmed my nose hair and headed off, prepared to charm. The restaurant he had chosen was not the sort of hip Manhattan eatery I was expecting. It had strange murals of an imagined Italian countryside on the walls and waiters that looked like they were putting the majority of their tips towards a hip replacement operation. If you had wanted to bring your mother out for a nice meal, this would have been perfect. Conversation at these sorts of things is always a bit stilted but we both soldiered on, asking each other first-date questions. 'Why move to the BBC?' he enquired.

I launched into my usual answer about having had enough of five nights a week but that going back to what I had been doing would seem like a retrograde step.

There was a pause. 'You mean like what I've done, coming back to Comedy Central?'

Well, he said it. I felt that was the end of any hope of a connection between us. Of course, this being American television, that didn't really matter. If the show was a hit, Doug Herzog would force himself to like me.

And so the PR machine cranked itself up until it was running full tilt. Posters for the show littered the city. I seemed to be on the side of every phone box and there was even a huge billboard on that highway I had travelled in on from the airport twenty years before.

The set was designed — we would be taping in Ricki Lake's old studio, which I had visited a few years earlier after I had met Ricki on my show. There is an episode about troubled teens who had been sent to a boot camp where my big, gormless face is in every shot as I sat in the audience next to Ms Lake conducting proceedings in the aisle. These studios then went on to be the home of a post-prison Martha Stewart. Oddly, the gay bar where Kristian would start his career as a drag queen was just across Seventh Avenue. That Small Apple again.

On the surface, everything was great, but behind the scenes things were proving more difficult. In Britain we had won BAFTAs and were used to being wined and dined by Channel 4 executives who trusted us to make the show the way we wanted. It was a shock to all our systems to be suddenly starting over and having to prove ourselves. The suits at Comedy Central just knew they were spending a lot of money on this import, so they wanted to make sure we got it right. That meant interference. Graham Stuart, my business partner, was the executive producer, while my long-time producer, Jon Magnusson, would continue doing his job, but it was decreed we needed something called a show runner.

Every American show has one of these and so we were duly given ours. He arrived in a ticker-tape parade of accolades. He had a fantastic comedy background and had worked on many hits on both coasts. Maybe it would be OK.

It was never going to be OK. In retrospect I feel sorry for the guy. He arrived in an office full of sullen toddlers who had been told they had to share their toys with the new kid. We stared at him and waited for the comedy magic.

My biggest problem with him was that he was wearing a wig. An obvious wig, but then on men I'm not sure there is any other kind. He might as well have just stuck an old bit of a car-seat cover on his head and left the house. I realise that people end up wearing wigs for many reasons. Perhaps he had gone bald very early and he wore it to try and prevent himself being bullied in school; maybe his wife preferred him with it perched on the northern slope of his forehead. My point was that if he could look in the mirror every morning before he left the house and fail to notice that he looked ridiculous, then I really didn't trust his comedy instincts. We stuck him for about ten days and then it was decided that he could stay on the payroll but work from home, and when we said 'work' we really meant 'stay'. If working in America was a learning curve, we seemed determined to walk in a straight line.

Booking guests is never easy, especially when your programme is the new kid on the block, but it looked like we had got Bette Midler for the first show. We were thrilled; Comedy Central less so. She was, we were told, the wrong 'demographic'. Apart from the obvious frustration we also felt a sense of foreboding. If the audience didn't like Bette then imagine how they would feel about the flamboyant homosexual with a funny accent — frankly, did it matter what guests we booked if the host was so wildly off-brand? Finally we were allowed to book the comedian and singer, Sandra Bernhard, and Marlon Wayans, one of the comedy-film-making brothers.

Over the series of thirteen shows, we managed to get a very respectable crop of celebrities to show up, including Sharon Stone, Anne Hathaway, Chris Rock, Jon Voight and Paul Rudd. As far as I'm aware, Jon Voight is the only guest on one of my shows to cry. It was nothing to do with any questions I asked, but he found he moved himself telling a story about his early days in New York so beautifully. We cut it.

The first show hit the ground running. The guests were great, the comedy items all worked and the audience in the studio went wild. We came off set pinching ourselves. This was a hit. A few of us went out for dinner afterwards and my agent Melanie wondered aloud what we would tell the BBC when our run got extended. The future seemed bright and very Manhattan-based.

Every year the various cable channels launch shows in the summer and there are what the industry call 'break-out' hits — shows that become so popular that they hit the mainstream. Shows like *Queer Eye for the Straight Guy, Here Comes Honey Boo Boo* or *Duck Dynasty* transformed the fortunes of the cable channels that broadcast them. *South Park*, first broadcast by Comedy Central in the summer of 1997, was the Holy Grail. Nobody thought we could duplicate that sort of success, but having spent quite a bit of money on getting us, they were hoping for some sort of hit.

The ratings were in — we were not the smash they had been looking for, but nor were we the sort of flop that would result in a mercy cancellation. Our figures were just a slight improvement on their usual Thursday-night audience. If we had been on one of the big networks we might have been stopped then and there, but cable is a little kinder. We could have our remaining three-month run and then a decision would be made.

Of course we hoped there would be a change in our fortunes, and the shows were some of the funniest and most outrageous we had ever made, but our figures just stuck where they were. Had we still been working with the people who had signed us to the channel we might have had a better chance of getting a second series but, as it was, one sensed that Doug Herzog was quite happy to be able to say goodbye to our show. I could put my Irish ass into reverse and go back to the UK where I belonged.

Someone must have been watching every week but I never met any of them. The only feedback I ever got was from the audience at the recordings. They loved it, but they sort of made it the most expensive off-Broadway show ever produced. The only other time anybody mentioned it was when I was buying some groceries from the small supermarket around the corner from my house.

The woman behind the till looked at me. 'You host that show on TV?'

I rearranged my features in preparation for the look of false modesty I was about to give her. 'Yes, I do.'

'I don't like it.'

As it happened, I didn't think she was doing a brilliant job bagging my orange juice and eggs, but you didn't hear me going on about it.

★　★　★

Having a smash hit in America must be wonderful, I imagine, but what we had was horrible. Comedy Central wanted a successful show but they had bought the wrong one. We were fighting a battle that was impossible to win. Hindsight is a marvellous, if completely useless, thing and I do believe that if we hadn't got so carried away in our meetings with the various channels and networks, we might have chosen a better home and had a modest success in the States. In Britain, the show had managed to drag my camp sensibility into the mainstream and we had thought we would be able to duplicate that in America. It would have been far wiser to embrace our niche audience and find a channel where they felt comfortable. In Britain, 'niche' or 'cult' equates with being small but of course, in America, because of its size, that can be enormous. Everything really is bigger there. Oddly, I don't remember feeling disappointed; I suppose we were all just happy the uphill struggle was over and grateful to have had a wonderful time living and partying in one of the world's greatest cities.

Occasionally I will get sucked back in and accept a job in New York — hosting the International Emmys, the GLAAD Media Awards or a panel show for BBC America called *Would You Rather . . .*? Every time the job is over I promise myself never to work in the city again. For me it is a place to live and enjoy, not somewhere I should or could ever make a living. It's hard to describe why I find it so difficult but it is something about the po-faced attitude and the language the people in the TV industry use. I recently agreed to talk to some American producers about hosting a show for them (I know — I refuse to learn!) and they emailed me the number I should call. The subject line read: Creative call with Graham Norton. I knew instantly I would be saying no to the job. Was someone else getting details for an *uncreative* call? It was the sort of meaningless executive speak I manage to avoid in the UK and it was all I needed to hear. That's a very mild example, but it illustrates a certain literal, 'worthy' quality that just sucks the joy out of a job that should be primarily fun. Perhaps when you are on the top of the entertainment heap in the States you get to mess around and have a laugh, but in the comedy foothills I inhabit it is pretty grim.

Now my relationship with New York is like that of one with a mistress: exciting, sexy and dangerous, but I'm always aware that I'm playing away. London is my life and Manhattan is my bit on the side. I rent my house out quite a lot now and probably only visit the city three or four times a year. Sometimes I head out to the Hamptons to stay with friends, but usually I try to make my trips coincide with when my little house is available. If I do nothing but sit on the roof terrace sipping a glass of wine, reading a book and listening to the sirens and roar of the dynamic fury that is the giant, glorious Apple, I feel like the journey has been worth it.

On a recent trip, I had the perfect New York night. Friends were in town and we went for dinner to the classic restaurant, Le Cirque. Dressed up in the smart jackets that we'd just bought that day, we enjoyed fabulous food and wine with a side dish of spectacular plastic surgery on display.

I had arranged to meet my friend, Eddie, for a Saturday night drink afterwards. As I left the restaurant he texted me to say that we were going to meet in Alan Cumming's dressing room at Studio 54, where he had just begun previews of the musical, *Cabaret*.

I adore Alan so was thrilled to get the chance to hang out with him. When I got to the top of the narrow backstage staircase, the room was thronged with well-wishers and friends. I knew most of them and, randomly, Matthew Morrison from *Glee* was amongst the crowd. I've interviewed him a couple of times, and he gave me the Broadway gossip while drinks magically appeared in our hands. Pretty soon, Alan declared we were going around the corner to meet some other people for drinks.

Down on the street, some people said their goodbyes and others got in a large black town car to travel the few blocks to the next haunt. Eddie and I decided to walk. We linked arms against a chill wind and headed off. We turned the corner into Times Square. If you have never been there, it is impossible to make you understand: it contains nothing more than enormous billboards and a lot of electricity; it is garish and commercial, and yet heart-stoppingly beautiful. The scale, colour and brightness of it all never fails to take my breath away. The world doesn't have a heart, of course, but if it did, I'm pretty sure it would feel like Times Square.

A few blocks further and we stumbled into the upstairs bar of the Broadway institution that is Sardi's. Alan's friends turned out to be Toni Collette with her husband, Dave; Michael C. Hall from *Dexter*; and Marisa Tomei. The three of them were in a play which was also previewing. Everyone was in high spirits, and appeared to be consuming them by the bucket-load. After about an hour, the nice people of Sardi's decided that while the city didn't sleep, they would quite like to, so we were asked to go on our way. Not to worry! There was another party down in Chelsea being held by the top agency for male models in the city. Who wouldn't want to go to that? We piled into taxis and headed south.

I found myself jammed into a back seat between Marisa and Eddie. For some reason I felt that there was an abnormal number of very famous people in Marisa's play and decided to share that view with the lady herself. I had a point and I was going to make it. She tried to argue but soon realised how strongly I felt about this issue and decided instead to just smile and nod for the remainder of our journey.

The outside of the bar was surrounded by a jostling throng. Someone unfamiliar with the clubbing scene of Manhattan might have thought people were fighting to get inside in order to get inoculated against a virulent fatal virus, rather than the reality of what waited on the other side of the doors — over-priced drinks being poured by people with way too much attitude to be in the service industry.

Eddie led us straight to the front of the line brandishing Marisa Tomei in front of him as our VIP pass. Unfortunately, our arrival at the rope coincided with a sudden surge from the crowd behind us.

'Get the fuck back!' the bouncer yelled into the very famous face in front of him.

We sucked the night air in through our clenched teeth. This wasn't good. Before Ms Tomei, whom I'm guessing hadn't been put in the best of moods by her taxi ride with me could say anything, Eddie intervened.

'Mmmm, I don't think you should — '

'Get the fuck back!' This was apparently the bouncer's mantra.

Happily, just then a woman with a clipboard hurried forward. Full of apologies, she pulled back the velvet rope and it was like the moment a film goes from black and white to colour. The bouncer turned into a charming teddy bear as if nothing bad had ever happened and he ushered us towards the VIP area.

The rest of us were simply relieved but Eddie couldn't let it go. Pointing at the top of Marisa Tomei's head like a child who had brought something special from home for Show and Tell, he looked up at the bouncer: 'She's won an Oscar!' Some wrongs must be righted. What's the point of the highest accolade the acting profession can bestow if it can't get you into a dark, sweaty bar? I doubt Meryl Streep has stood in a line for anything since 1979.

I tell this story not because it's amazing or special but simply because it is the latest random night I've had in New York and it's the sort of evening anyone can so easily have in the city. You may not have an Alan Cumming or an Eddie to sprinkle celebrity on your story, but you will meet the guy with the skateboard who invites you to the apartment with no bathroom and fifteen parrots, where the drunk woman shows you her tattoo of George Michael . . . I don't know what it is but things happen here. When So Television had the office in New York, Monday mornings would be a list of what everyone had done over the weekend — rollerblading in the park, followed by brunch with fifteen people and then a friend's birthday party with a Sunday full of exhibitions and movies. The same conversation back home would have just consisted of: 'We bought some towels and watched *The X Factor*.'

New York may be too much for me to keep up with full time, but dipping into it occasionally gives me as big a jolt as pissing on an electric fence only it's a good thing and my penis doesn't turn blue. The nights out, the shopping, the musicals, the hot spots, the celebrities — it's all nonsense and yet in New York it does really feel like it matters. The world has a core and it's inside a great big apple — shiny, delicious and so big you can never take too many bites out of it. I heart New York.

4

Divas

I was in a bar in New York recently (there's a surprise) when two boys approached me (that *was* a surprise). They were visiting the city from Atlanta and wanted to tell me how much they liked my show on BBC America. I thanked them and then, when they asked for a photo, got one of my friends to take it. They seemed pleased, one of them confiding, 'I'm so glad you were nice. The last time we were in the city we were walking down Fifth Avenue and we saw Madonna. We got all excited and started to tell her how much we love her. She never slowed down — just turned her head as she passed, flicked her hair, and said, 'Hi and bye'.'

Were they really upset? Isn't that how they wanted their goddess to behave? The star that stops for photos and a chat is Sally Field or, closer to home, Fern Britton — not Madonna. We want our divas to behave like . . . well, divas.

Please don't misunderstand me. The word 'diva' is much over-used. In the same way that phrases like 'gay icon' or 'national treasure' simply mean 'unemployed has-been', so too 'diva' is used, too often, to simply describe a rude bitch. If you have to demand it, you are second rate. There are hundreds of rude bitches out there, but to my mind there are very few true divas.

Being a diva isn't just an attitude; it's something that's been earned over the years by being special. It is a quality that exists due to a strange combination of talent and permission.

★ ★ ★

We had finished our lunch shift at Smiths, the restaurant I was working in, and had wandered over from Covent Garden towards Leicester Square. The year was 1985 and we were on our way to see the film *Desperately Seeking Susan*. I was aware of Madonna from 'Holiday' and 'Like a Virgin', but she was no more to me than Cyndi Lauper or Belinda Carlisle were — I assume we were seeing the movie because of good reviews, or perhaps a friend had told us about it. With no preconceptions, myself; my waitress friend, Nicky; and my first proper boyfriend, Ashley, from Australia, settled into the warm darkness of the cinema and waited for the screen to come alive.

We loved it — very funny, lots of scenes in New York and a life-changing sequence with Aidan Quinn in a pair of sweat pants.

That image lived in my mind for many years, until I saw him recently in *Elementary*, the American version of *Sherlock*. Time has not been kind. It makes you very aware of the danger of answered prayers — if God had listened to me in 1985 I would now be sharing a bed with a lumbering older gentleman with no obvious physical charms. It reminded me of my mother having lunch with 'the girls' one day after Tony Curtis had appeared on my show, bloated and bald. Back in the day, when they had been saving pennies to get a new lipstick, Mr Curtis had caused their young hearts to flutter wildly. Around the lunch table, comparing how he had turned out in relation to the home-grown lads they had married, there was a general consensus that they hadn't done too badly.

When the movie ended, I remember not wanting the lights in the auditorium to come up — I wanted to stay in that world for ever. Not because of Aidan or Rosanna Arquette, but because I never wanted to let go of Madonna.

Over the years it has become fairly obvious that she may not be God's gift to the craft of acting, but when it comes to being Madonna she can do it better than anyone else. She is so convinced she is special that we are all swept along. A tsunami of ambition and need, she is almost literally irresistible. Given the huge, catering-sized turkeys she has delivered at the movies, I approached Alan Parker's film version of *Evita* with a certain amount of trepidation . . . I watched the opening scenes with Antonio Banderas singing about 'moaning all day, moaning all night', and my worst fears were realised.

Enter Madonna.

She shames the rest of the cast. Her commitment and belief is so great it carries the whole movie. She is Evita because she is Madonna, a woman who willed herself to be successful because for her, success was the ultimate goal, not what got you there. I felt that year they should have given Madonna a special Oscar for that once-in-a-lifetime contribution to cinema. It's not unprecedented — they gave one to Lassie.

And while the other disco queens came and went, Madonna stubbornly refused to leave the limelight. She used whatever means necessary to stay there: the romances, the videos, her book of photographs with the understated title *Sex*.

I'm not sure why but I decided, even though it had been banned in Ireland, to buy my sister and brother-in-law that book for Christmas. I remember it being opened and the blank stares all round, their 'thank you's sounding more like questions than statements. Maybe I was just hoping they'd say they didn't want it and give it to me. I wonder where it is now. I imagine it is languishing in a damp corner of a disused milking parlour. As my father would have said, 'That's probably worth something now.'

For the younger reader it is hard to describe the impact a song like 'Vogue' had on the parochial gay world in London. Madonna may have borrowed the dance craze from the gay ballrooms of Harlem and taken it mainstream, but she never pretended that it was anything less than uber gay. I remember back in 1990 standing in the Vauxhall Tavern, just south of the bridge in London, when the staff pulled down the projection screen that hung from the ceiling at the front of the small stage that usually played host to great drag acts like the much-missed

Regina Fong or the acerbic wonder of Lily Savage. In washed-out colour they played us a shaky videotape of Madonna's performance at that year's MTV Awards. Clutching our warm pints of lager we stared with incredulity. Performing the song in the style of *Les Liaisons Dangereuses*, she referenced oral sex, drug use and had dancers who didn't just seem gay — that was the point of them. Standing in that little bar in south London, it seemed amazing that this was happening on a world stage. We didn't feel like she was using us, or pandering to us — this was a celebration. People born after a certain point will never understand the devotion of gay men to a select few performers, but in a time before gay weddings and mainstream

'out' lesbian and gay entertainers, they were the ones who openly acknowledged our existence. We felt included. Yes, the community had embraced Madonna, but she was making very sure everyone knew she was hugging us back. At a time when we only saw ourselves reflected on a screen or page when it was in reference to AIDS, here was somebody urging us to dance. We happily obliged.

At the Fridge nightclub in Brixton, the coolest night was called the Daisy Chain and the hottest boys stayed on the dance floor all night towards the front, near the stage. Sometimes wearing top hats, sometimes wearing very little else, they Vogued. We wanted to hate them but they were so sexy and, in that moment, unbelievably cool.

At a meeting a couple of years ago, I was introduced to someone who would be working on the project in which I was involved. I stared at him for at least half an hour and then it came to me. 'Did you ever Vogue at the Fridge?'

A strange expression of embarrassment and pride flickered across the man's face. 'Yes.'

I got that sinking Aidan Quinn feeling and I quietly thanked God that I have never been hot. It makes getting older a great deal easier.

★ ★ ★

When *So Graham Norton* started on Channel 4 in 1998 I made a list of all the guests I wanted. Top of that list was Madonna. Over the years, every other name on that roll call made their way to my sofa: Dolly, Cher, Liza, Bette, but it was to be fourteen long years till I finally got to say, 'Ladies and gentlemen, please welcome Madonna.' Just typing that I got goose bumps. Tragic, but not as tragic as some of the things I did over the years to try and endear myself to the great lady and make her accept one of my umpteen invitations. In 2001, after a taping of the show, I and a few people who worked on the programme went to a charity auction. Jonathan Ross was hosting and Hear'Say were the entertainment (which gives you some sense of how long ago it was). One of the lots up for auction was a small photograph of Madonna's eyes taken by the acclaimed photographer, Herb Ritts. We were told it had formerly hung in her LA mansion. I decided that if I bought it, word would get back and she'd feel honour-bound to come and chat.

A little drunk and encouraged by my friends, I started to bid. Unbeknownst to me, the other main bidder was one of the richest men in Britain. We soon left hundreds of pounds behind us and were shooting through the thousands. Happily, the other man was a bit more sober than I was and bowed out, leaving me to fork out £10,000 for my little photo. As Cher said when she heard what I'd paid: 'Are you out of your fucking mind? You could have got her actual eyes for that!'

Of course it didn't work and my begging continued to be ignored. At least the event wasn't a complete waste of time and money, though, since I learnt that night never to drink at an auction. I assume Sara Cox also woke up the next morning with that truism etched on her brain: she paid £4,000 for a Swan Lake outfit from the movie of *Billy Elliot*. I wonder where that is now? Madonna's eyes for many years hung in my bedroom, but recently they've been moved into my bathroom. I'm not sure which view I'd like to see less.

There were a few close calls over the years: 'Could you do an interview in a hotel?'

'We don't do that.'

And:

'Madonna would like to talk about her book.'

'We're not back on air till later in the year!'

In every interview I ever did, when people asked me who I wanted on the show, like a gay parrot I immediately squawked, 'Madonna!'

Towards the end of the summer in 2011 we began to get whispers that perhaps she was finally ready to perch her perfectly toned buttocks on the edge of our red couch. The conditions began. It had to be a special. Yes. She wants to tape it in the afternoon. Yes. She wants approval over the music. Yes. I wonder how far we would have gone? What demand could have provoked a no? I couldn't think of one.

None of the producers or members of the production team were nearly as keen as I was but, at the same time, they knew how special this would be for me. While my whole life is my dream come true, it was still a wildly exciting moment for me and, in *my* head at least, for the show as well. It was the royal seal of approval.

A few weeks before the day of the taping I received an invitation to a champagne reception at Claridge's that would be followed by a screening of Madonna's directorial debut, *W.E.* Obviously I was going to go and no further incentive was needed, but I was also told, strictly confidentially, that this would be the moment when I finally met her.

No audience with the Pope or Queen could have made me more nervous or excited. I've never understood people who ask for autographs and pictures, or who spend hours peering through the railings at the back of the television studios where we tape, but the night of the reception, despite my fancy clothes and champagne, I was one of them.

Happily, there were a few people I knew there and I chatted with them to distract me from what was about to happen. The ornate room had started to fill up with a mixture of media people and celebrities. No one was sure if she was there or not but suddenly the door opened and every eye in the place swivelled towards it. The eagle had landed.

Trying not to stare, we all stared. Madonna made her way into the room shaking hands and making brief small talk, like the Queen visiting a toothbrush factory in Sheffield.

A woman in a dark suit appeared at my shoulder. 'Come with me.'

My mouth went dry and I followed. We moved through the sea of bodies till we reached the shining island at the centre of the throng.

'Madonna, this is Graham Norton.'

'Hello.' A pale hand was extended towards me. I shook it and took a closer look at the face. Blonde hair worn in loose waves, eyes bright, smile wide, she looked healthy and happy and nothing like the cosmetic confection I had been fearing.

'Congratulations on the film.'

'Oh, have you seen it already?'

'No, I'm seeing it tonight.'

'Well, save your congratulations till afterwards.'

Oh, for fuck's sake! Seconds in and it was all going wrong. I tried to explain that I was merely congratulating her because I knew how hard she had worked on the production. This seemed to placate her and we talked about her upcoming appearance on the show for a few moments before she was moved on to talk to the next loser.

Someone must have taken a photograph of us during our brief exchange because I have it framed in my house. We're both grinning, but I'm the one holding a drink and looking about ten years older than her.

I walked back to my friends and the only word I could think of to describe how I felt was 'high'. After a few moments, the euphoria started to pass and I longed to meet her again. If this is what happens to the people wearing dandruff-drenched anoraks waiting outside theatres and studios, no wonder they come back for more. The contact high from your idols turns out to be addictive.

I am aware how crazy this sounds. Over the years I have met a ridiculous number of celebrities, some of whom I admire hugely, but this wasn't just about the star. It was the journey that had led me to that moment in that room. I hadn't fully understood how desperately I had been seeking Madonna, but the effect of that handshake suggested that I had passed some sort of life milestone I hadn't even known I had been heading towards.

★　★　★

The night before the taping of the show I went to bed consciously thinking, 'This is Madonna eve,' and the first thing that entered my mind when I woke the next morning was, 'This is Madonna day!'

Normally, friends rarely come to the studio to watch a recording but there was going to be a big turn-out that day, I knew. I was never so acutely aware that they were not there to see me. The whole building had a special buzz: security men standing where none had been before, windows blacked out, dressing rooms double-checked.

Like all the really big old-school stars, Madonna arrived with a very small entourage — just hair, make-up and a couple of PR people. The celebrities who last the course work out very quickly that while it may be nice to have an enormous crowd of people fawning over you, they all need to be paid and that it is your money. The sign of a true great is having a tiny team who have worked with them for years. Madonna has that.

It might have been an afternoon taping but the atmosphere in the studio was thick with anticipation and love. And then finally, *finally*, I was saying out loud: 'Ladies and gentlemen, please welcome Madonna!' and there she was.

It was really happening.

The rest of the show is sort of a blur. I remember being nervous and then both of us relaxing. We got the measure of each other.

Some fans had flown in from Italy with a series of extremely detailed and well-made dolls of their idol in various famous outfits she had worn over the years — a similar thing happened when Lady Gaga was on the show. Gaga went into the audience and hugged the Japanese lady who had made them. How different the reaction of the material girl. She peered at the dolls like someone whose cat has just delivered a half-eaten mouse at their feet and then proceeded to point out the mistakes in the various outfits.

Even I felt a bit sorry for the boys and when I saw them after the show, I tried to apologise for Madonna's reaction, but there was no need. They were delighted. The queen of their world had reacted just as they knew and hoped she would. It was Fifth Avenue all over again, and we were dealing with a diva.

A short time afterwards, we were busy having a debrief in the office when I got word that I was wanted upstairs. I ran. I found her and her 'people' making their way down a corridor.

'Thank you so much!' I gushed.

I began trying to pay her more compliments when she interrupted. 'I just wanted to say bye,' she said, doing her very best impression of a regular person. But then, with no words being exchanged, someone came up behind her and slipped her into a fur coat, proving she was anything but.

No friendship developed. She remained the icy star, me the awe-struck fan boy, our worlds never to collide. We've only met once more but, oddly, under circumstances that couldn't have been more different or personal.

Madonna and I shared a good friend. His name was David Collins, a hugely successful and highly respected interior designer. I had met him briefly at various parties but really got to know him when we happened to be on holiday in Cape Town at the same time. He, too, came from Ireland but had made his life in the UK. Before one can list any of David's qualities — his generosity, his style, his thoughtfulness — one has to say he was funny. To meet him was to laugh. Often it was quite barbed, but maybe that's why I liked him so very much. Initially, he never mentioned Madonna in conversation but then he didn't need to because mutual friends were full of tales of their close friendship. Over time, he did occasionally speak about her and he even tried to introduce us on a few occasions but, for various reasons, it never happened.

Neither of us could have guessed that when David finally brought us together, it would be at his funeral.

That day is not mine to talk about in these pages. It belongs to David's family and all of us who loved him, but I do want to describe one moment at the lunch after the service. We were all sitting in a hotel dining room looking out at the sun-soaked Wicklow Mountains. It should

129

have been the setting for a wedding or a birthday, not the farewell to a friend, brother and son who had left so suddenly and far too soon.

There had been rumours that Madonna was going to attend the funeral. While part of me wanted her to be there because it would have meant so much to David, I was also aware that her presence could easily dominate the whole day and take the attention away from him and his family.

We were just sitting down to lunch, still shell-shocked by what was happening, when someone asked if Madonna was going to appear.

'She's here,' said a woman at our table, and pointed across the room. Star wattage turned down to zero, there she was, dressed simply and making conversation with the other mourners. There was no sense that she was incognito or in disguise, she just understood that this day was not about her. After the meal she got up to speak. Again I have no right to report the things she said but what struck me was that this wasn't a global superstar, or the woman who had snarled on Fifth Avenue: this was someone who had lost her friend and who spoke simply and sincerely. She expressed everything we were feeling, and gave the hideously premature goodbye just the right mix of emotion and occasion.

People can try to downplay Madonna and her talent and often it is hard to argue with them, but one simple fact is undeniable — she is Madonna. A star for thirty years, still making hits and causing controversy, she's even in the *Oxford English Dictionary*. That isn't a reward for dancing, singing or changing her hairstyle — it is down to hard work and a single-minded vision. She could have chosen sport or politics, but she opted for entertainment and built a ladder from spit and determination to the very top.

That afternoon in Ireland, I saw that she still knew the woman who had started the climb on the bottom rung. Madonna. Long may she reign over us.

★ ★ ★

My big break nearly broke me. Twenty-seven episodes in ten days left me feeling like I should have been digging coal or finding a cure for cancer, not being the sidekick on a late-night, sex-based quiz called *Carnal Knowledge*. As far as I'm aware, two good things came from it, however: firstly, my friendship with its host, Maria McErlane, who has remained a very close friend — we still work together on my Radio 2 show during the 'Grill Graham' segment, when we attempt to help listeners with their problems; and secondly, far more surprising — my agent was contacted by the production company saying that they'd received a call from someone trying to buy the American rights to the show.

That person was Cher.

Obviously I wasn't a complete idiot. I did understand that if something was broadcast on television some people would see it; but this wasn't people, this was Cher. Apparently she was living in London at the time, recording her

131

album *Believe*, and was having trouble sleeping. In a time before Sky and Freeview, her options were limited and so she had been stuck with me and Maria helping drunk couples draw their favourite sexual positions on a blackboard. At the time, we were told she was renting a penthouse in the Docklands area but I have since discovered she was in the block of warehouse apartments that are next door to where I live. Like a salmon heading home to spawn, I've been mystically drawn to the sacred spot.

We waited to hear more. Maybe Cher would jet us all to America or maybe Cher would never call back and we wouldn't hear anything about it ever again . . . ?

I think you know what happened.

Fast-forward two years to 1998, my chat show was on the air and I and my then boyfriend, Scott, were in the cavernous gay club, Heaven, one Saturday night. We trawled around the various bars and then waited for that night's show to begin, whatever it might be.

As I surveyed the crowd, one small, grey-haired figure caught my eye.

'Is that . . . it can't be . . . is that Judi Dench?' We both studied the woman standing in the crowd. It certainly looked very like the great dame. Then I noticed a bald man near the stage who bore an uncanny resemblance to Sir Ben Kingsley. What on earth was going on?

Soon the lights dimmed, and a voice urged us all to welcome to the stage the one and only . . . Cher!

That we did! The roar echoed through the old

railway arches and then, without further ado, there she was. Where many a Cher impersonator had stood before, here now was the real thing — the microphone held with a pinky finger in the air, a long, thin, false nail pulling errant strands of wig off her face. We felt like competition winners.

Her mouth forming perfect Os, Cher told us she was going to perform her new single. She hadn't had a hit for a while but that didn't matter. We would happily sway along to whatever bland disco-lite music she wanted to play for us.

The track started and our ears pricked up. This was different. The song was 'Believe' and it is still one of the highest-selling singles of all time, topping the charts in over twenty countries. We were just two people amongst the thousands there that night and yet somehow I felt a personal connection, not just to Cher, but also the song. That Christmas, I went with Scott back to his native Detroit and whenever 'Believe' came on in a bar, I felt like I knew a secret. I guess that is just something that happens with those sorts of songs. They aren't just an earworm; they are a hardwired connection to places and people. A few years later, I was standing with a herd of cows in Mozambique, waiting to cross a river as part of a Comic Relief project. A group of locals were arguing about how best to organise the crossing when the little shack by the side of the road started blaring out Cher's 'Believe'. We hear the expression a lot, but that is what 'world famous' must mean. Under the unforgiving African sun, and over the distressed mooing of the cattle, her unmistakable voice rang out telling us all about love, and how much she believed in it.

* * *

It was the fourth series of *So Graham Norton* when Cher agreed to come on the show. By that time we had had quite a few big names and heroes of mine but I was still desperate for her to like me, or at the very least, not make me hate her.

She arrived with remarkably little fuss, and chatted to me and the audience like we were old friends. She has been doing this for quite a while and one gets the impression she is very comfortable in her own skin. Unlike some of the younger stars, she isn't worried about her 'demographic' or her 'image'. If you ask her a question she doesn't like, or suggest she takes part in something she doesn't fancy, she'll just tell you to fuck off and then move on with no hard feelings.

After that first encounter, all people wanted to know was what she looked like up close. In truth she doesn't look her age but neither does she look as stretched and plumped as you might imagine. A lot of that incredibly smooth skin is achieved by wearing an almost *kabuki* quantity of white make-up that reflects the light. She is by no means prune-like, but I can report there are a few wrinkles. Cher herself is refreshingly frank about getting older. She hates that when people say to her, 'You look great,' she knows that hanging silent in the air is the unspoken, ' . . . for your age.' The other thing that frustrates her is that everyone assumes that how she looks is all down to the surgeon's knife and various cosmetic cheats, when in fact she spends hours at the gym and works extremely hard to look the way she does.

She has now been on the show four times and every time I am struck by how unconcerned she seems to be by the cult of Cher. I think she enjoys the attention and she certainly takes pleasure in her career longevity. There is a song in the movie *Burlesque*, written for her by Diane Warren, that sums her up perfectly: 'You Haven't Seen the Last of Me'. She is also always far more interested in talking about other people's projects or the current state of politics; I'm not a huge fan of Twitter but joining it is worth it just to read Cher's random rants, which all appear to be written in the middle of the night. I guess she still has trouble sleeping.

Dawn French was one of the other guests on the couch for one of Cher's appearances. The three of us got on well and afterwards Dawn and I thought it would be only polite to pop into Cher's dressing room to say goodbye. We found her sitting in her make-up chair and apparently in no rush to leave. She wanted to talk. The subject turned to British comedy and we were astonished to find that this American legend had an almost encyclopaedic knowledge of various shows we had done. She was talking about *French and Saunders* sketches that I had to confess I had no recollection of. She still remembered *Carnal*

Knowledge from all those years ago, but also knew my episodes of *Father Ted*.

I know it shouldn't be surprising to find a superstar who is obsessed by things besides themselves, but I'm here to tell you that it is extremely rare. Our quick goodnight turned into a chat lasting over an hour and Dawn French and I found ourselves in the ridiculous position of trying to make our excuses and get out of the dressing room of one of our heroes.

Downstairs, reality quickly reasserted itself. My friends had gone and upstairs, in my dressing room, Madge had failed to fully control her bladder. I refer to my dog, not the aforementioned diva.

At the end of 2013 Cher was back with a new album, *Closer to the Truth*, and was busy planning a tour. She was in a great mood and seemed to be relishing the prospect of performing once more and feeling the love. She attempted a Vegas residency but I'm not sure how much she enjoyed it. Normally when she tours the crowd goes crazy and their energy and love is infectious, but in Vegas, because of the ticket prices and the sort of people who go to the shows attached to casinos, she found herself struggling. The minute she walked on stage she could see the rows of grey hair, the people who were attached to oxygen tanks, and should somebody find the sudden spurt of energy required to jump up and dance, an usher promptly told them to sit down. She told me the only way she got through it was by giving herself a little pep talk before she went on stage: 'This may well be the last concert some of these folks will ever see. Let's make it a good one!'

The night after Cher chatted and performed on the show, teasing Robert De Niro and behaving like a fan girl with Dawn's partner-in-crime Jennifer Saunders, I had been asked to present the great lady with an award. The gay magazine *Attitude* holds a glamorous dinner every year and for Cher, they had invented a special Legend Award. It was to be the final one of the evening. The event was being held in the Royal Courts of Justice in London, and the combination of the glitz of the evening and the gothic architecture of the building seemed like the perfect setting for Cher. I sort of enjoy random nights like this where you have no idea who you might meet. I took my friend, Roger, and we got lucky, spending most of our time chatting with Daniel Radcliffe and the rugby star, Ben Cohen, who was there with his lovely wife, Abbie. Happily we managed to avoid the Speaker of the House of Commons, John Bercow, and his wife, Sally.

I had always assumed that John was slightly saddled with the embarrassment of being married to Sally but, that night, I discovered they truly do deserve each other. John got up to read the citation for an award winner and for some reason best known to himself, spoke for forty minutes. Unforgiveable — not just for boring the arse off everyone, but also because he was keeping Cher waiting.

She had arrived about halfway through proceedings and was being kept in a wood-panelled room in another part of the building. I

137

don't know if it was where one would usually find twelve angry men, but on this night it was home to one miserable diva. I was led through the stone corridors and staircases till I stood outside her door. A timid knock and in I went. The other people in the room spoke in whispers and across the wide expanse of a polished wooden table sat Cher. She smiled weakly and beckoned me over.

'I'm so sick.' And she clearly was. Apparently, after doing my show she had started to feel ill and she had woken up feeling even worse. She had wanted to cancel but felt she couldn't let people down, particularly knowing that tonight was about her core audience. I reminded her of something she had said sixteen years earlier on stage at Heaven: 'You guys have kept me in beads for years.' It was her unsentimental way of saying thank you to the people who had continued to buy her music and go to her concerts when she was no longer fashionable.

She nodded, and started in her low rasp of a voice to talk about how gay men had entered her life from a very young age. Her mother had had two hairdresser friends who used to visit their house, much to the delight of the little girl that would become Cher. She told me that for years she thought the word 'gay' just meant fun.

Introducing the award, knowing that Cher was listening to me, I reminded the audience that while we were loyal to her, she had also been very loyal to us. At various times in the past when the gay community didn't have many friends, she stood up for us, and she stood by us.

138

The wigs, the feathers, the sailors on the gun ship — clearly it is all very camp and silly, and while some people with hearts of chalk will always rush to dismiss it, for the rest of us, it is something to be celebrated and cherished. Somehow Cher has taken the summer of love and made it last a lifetime. Thank you.

★　★　★

The summer of 1982 was when I did a lot of growing up. It was the end of my first year at university and I'd flown to Paris. My parents imagined I was heading off to practise my French and get a job, but in reality I was following my thirty-seven-year-old French lecturer to the city of love for a clandestine affair. My levels of sophistication were off the scale.

Before you make some obvious assumptions, I should point out that the professor in question was female. Sadly, our sex-fuelled adventure was short-lived. After one too many arguments, she accused me of being gay and slept with someone else. I'm still not sure why we needed to travel all the way to Paris for her to spot the fact that I was not God's gift to the world of heterosexuality. At the time, I didn't want to admit it to myself, but I'm fairly sure for someone who was nearly forty there were clues a-plenty.

Newly single, I stormed off into the night and spent a few days wandering around the city like a rosy-cheeked ghost. I spoke to no one and quickly decided that I'd be better off in London, where I knew some people and could actually speak the language.

I know I only spent two or maybe three afternoons by myself in Paris but in the faded newsreel of my memory it feels like weeks. Hours spent sitting by the Seine drinking red wine out of a plastic bottle; a morning watching the buskers outside the Pompidou Centre, desperate to join in but not sure how. At some point in my short solo sojourn, I went to a cinema to see the movie *Cabaret*.

It was the perfect film for me to see at exactly that moment in my life. I should, of course, have been identifying with Michael York's character, Brian — an innocent abroad in a foreign city, struggling with his sexuality, but it was in Liza Minnelli's Sally Bowles that I saw myself most clearly: desperate for love and fame but without a clue how to find either one of them. There is an extraordinary sequence in the film after Sally has an abortion. Brian begs her to tell him why. The film cuts to an 'inner monologue' of images that wordlessly explains to the viewer why she had to terminate the baby, but to Brian she just shrugs her shoulders, unable to articulate her feelings. I found myself in tears but in a way that suggested I was crying for a great deal more than some movie character's misfortune. Just like Sally, my brittle bravado couldn't disguise how out of my depth I felt. The garish lights and anthemic songs failing to mask the dark air of menace, it finally dawned on me how lonely and full of fear for the future I was.

Realising that not all endings are happy was a very sobering thought for the young Irish boy who had always just assumed that things would work out for the best. When Sally's heart was broken, so was mine.

Liza Minnelli is in fact a freak. Talent oozes from her every pore. Singing, acting, dancing — she is exceptional at all of them. Only fifteen people have an Emmy, Grammy, Oscar and Tony award: Liza Minnelli is one of them. You might think that sort of ability would make a performer seem invincible or superhuman, but Liza is almost the exact opposite; so vulnerable that at any moment she might melt away like the witch her mother so famously destroyed years before. It's as if her gifts weigh her down rather than support her. The voice that is about to crack, the eyes welling with tears, the limbs about to tumble. She is perpetually raw and that must surely be some sort of curse.

Over the years I remained a fan but not so loyal or devoted that I didn't laugh along with everyone else when the drag superstar Adrella did her Liza act at the Vauxhall Tavern, face covered in a mystery white powder. Apart from a brief renaissance with the Pet Shop Boys and their brilliant version of Sondheim's 'Losing My Mind', Liza Minnelli seemed to be lost to us. The only pictures we saw were when she was leaving a hospital in a wheelchair, or some paparazzo got a shot of her looking very far from her best. I confess I didn't think about it a great deal, but when I did, I just assumed she was the victim of a talent and a legacy that was too much for her to bear.

Enter David Gest. I have met this man several

141

times but his mystery remains intact. All I know for sure is that he is some sort of producer and he had childhood links to Michael Jackson. In 2001 he announced that he was producing two concerts in New York with a host of superstars to celebrate Michael Jackson's thirtieth anniversary in music. They were going to be Jackson's first shows for eleven years and there was huge anticipation.

I remember feeling, like many, that they were bound to be a disaster. As it turned out, they were anything but. MJ was no longer the handsome youth who had introduced the world to the Moonwalk, but he could still do it, and well. Elizabeth Taylor introduced his brothers to the stage for a reunion, Whitney Houston performed, Britney Spears joined in, Marlon Brando spoke. David Gest had pulled a spectacular rabbit out of a weird, misshapen hat. CBS Television taped the second concert and it was set to make a global impact. It was 10 September 2001. It's all about timing.

In the middle of all the preparations for the concert, David Gest had decided that bringing Michael Jackson back to the stage wasn't enough. He phoned Liza Minnelli.

Perhaps he didn't know that the year before, she had contracted viral encephalitis so badly that doctors had told her she wouldn't walk again — there had even been fears she might lose the ability to speak. People can say what they like about David, and in fairness he is undeniably creepy, but like Jesus with a sequin-covered Lazarus, he brought Liza back from the dead.

142

So far so good. Up to that point in the story, everyone just thought that he was a talented and persuasive producer, but then David announced that he and Liza were getting married. The world scratched its head.

Before any wedding bells would ring out, however, we were told that Liza was returning to the stage. She would perform four concerts at the Royal Albert Hall. The excitement of gay men of a certain age was matched only by their concern about her ability to actually deliver the goods. Was David pushing her too far, too fast? Maybe it would be kinder just to put his cash cow out to pasture?

My show *V Graham Norton* was now on five nights a week, so the quality of the guests varied wildly. Booking a legend like Liza Minnelli was therefore a very big deal for us. Sadly, the price for securing the appearance of such an icon was that David Gest would have to appear too.

To say Mr Gest is not televisually friendly would be an understatement. He looks like a toddler has been given free rein to draw a face on an egg with a black marker pen. The sunglasses help. Clearly a surgeon has been involved but one gets the impression that there was a flashing red neon sign in the window saying: 'Low Low Prices'. A couple of friends of mine were having dinner with David in London when he suddenly said to the younger of the two, 'How old do you think I am?' My poor friend stared at him. Was there a right answer to this question? Numbers from thirty-five to eighty bounced around his brain. Finally, he plucked at one of them. 'Fifty?' It was impossible to decipher what expression might have been on Mr Gest's face. His mouth moved. It seemed to be a smile. 'Well, I'm fifty-one, so I guess the surgery was worth it.' David is living proof of the old adage that there are two areas where you don't look for a bargain: sushi and plastic surgery.

Having never seen Liza in the flesh I wasn't sure what to expect, but she looked great. She had lost weight, was full of energy and, compared to some chat show appearances I had seen, she seemed coherent and in full possession of her anecdotes. Of course she talked about 'Mama', that constant presence that she will have to haul around with her for as long as she lives. Liza told a cute story about when Judy Garland had called her to invite her to her last wedding. Due to some work commitments Liza couldn't go and, without thinking, blurted down the phone: 'I'm so sorry, Mama, but I promise I'll come to the next one!'

David sat beside her and the two of them seemed almost skittish together. It was beyond comprehension, but they appeared to make each other very happy. Towards the end of the interview Liza announced she had a surprise for me and handed over an envelope. I assumed it would be tickets for her concert. I ripped open the envelope and found in my hand an invitation to their wedding! If Tom Cruise had asked me to watch him have a back, sack and crack, I couldn't have been more excited. I decided to save a little money on postage: 'Yes!'

The invitation now sits framed in my kitchen. It has lasted a lot longer than the marriage but back in 2002, who could have guessed things wouldn't work out? In case you can't guess, the answer to that question is: 'Everyone. Everyone guessed.'

Shortly after the shiny new couple had been on the show, I got a call from my agent: 'David Gest wants you to introduce Liza at the Royal Albert Hall.'

Again it was a no-brainer: 'Yes!' I liked the idea that I would be the answer to a really obscure quiz for the most devout Liza Minnelli fans.

Being backstage on the opening night was an extraordinary privilege. Obviously there was a sense of excitement and anticipation, but there was also a great deal of fear as 5,000 people, mostly gay men of a certain age, took their seats and hoped that their idol could still do this.

In her dressing room, the idol didn't seem so sure. For a reason I never discovered there hadn't been a full run-through of the show, never mind a dress rehearsal. If Liza got to the finish line, it would be a miracle.

The lights went down and the audience was immediately disappointed: I was introduced. I realised that this crowd only wanted to hear about one thing and that was Liza with a zeeeee! I obliged and tried to build the sense of occasion. Finally, when I thought they had been made to wait long enough, I introduced the living legend.

The noise was like nothing I had heard before. It was a pure, vocal outpouring of love. This woman they thought they would never see again was back and these people wanted to make sure she knew how happy that made them.

I watched the show from a box to one side of the stage and was as captivated as everyone else. Sure, there were ropey sections and she wasn't the mover or vocalist she had been, but the whole evening was worth it for the moment when she sang a little snatch from 'Somewhere Over the Rainbow' for the first time in public.

I'm sure there are those who couldn't have cared less but, that night, myself and the rest of the crowd in that hall were thrilled to our very core. At the end, the ovation seemed to go on for ever. Had she wanted to, Liza could have surfed on the waves of love rolling and crashing onto the stage.

When she finally said goodbye, I waited for a while before heading back to her dressing room. I imagined it would be thronged with David and an adoring entourage. I stood in front of her door. Silence. Nobody waiting and, by the sounds of it, nobody inside either. It transpired David was keeping everyone in some sort of holding area so that Ms Minnelli would make an appearance later. I knocked.

'Come in.'

Inside she was sitting, all alone, at her dressing table, her face glistening and fresh with a combination of make-up remover and sweat. She looked up at me with eyes the size of paddling pools and I was transported back to 1982 in that French cinema and the scene where Liza opens the door and holds up her unvarnished nails to declare, 'Hands of an angel.'

I rushed forward to tell her how brilliant she had been. Superlatives poured out of my mouth like a treacle waterfall.

She grabbed my hand and pleaded, 'Did I do OK?'

I realised then that she wasn't fishing for more compliments — it was just that even the roars of approval of 5,000 people had not been enough. We all know that performers can have insecurities, but this was taking things to a new level. She required even more validation and extra love. A friend of mine once described Liza Minnelli as a 'vortex of need' and, in that moment, I witnessed it. David Gest was taking on an impossible task.

* * *

The press was full of who had been invited to the wedding. As well as me, she had invited the model Helena Christensen, whom she had met on my show; the former Spice Girl, Mel C, who had moved tables for Liza and David in some nightclub; and Martine McCutcheon, who had met the happy couple twice. Martine was a bridesmaid.

I had a plus one but since I was single at the time I hadn't known who to bring. It was a bit of an extreme first date. In the end I had the inspired idea of asking my good friend, Carrie Fisher. This wedding was going to be the stuff of showbiz legend and it seemed only right that the daughter of Debbie Reynolds and icon in her own right, thanks to *Star Wars*, should be there.

The weekend got off to a dramatic start when the Concorde hurtling down the runway at Heathrow suddenly screeched to a halt and we were all brought back to the terminal. The crash that had killed over 100 Concorde passengers had happened in the summer of 2000 and the planes had only been back in service for four months when we had our incident. This was big news, especially because the flight was packed with journalists heading over to cover the wedding of the century. Bizarrely for Concorde, which regularly had royalty on board, I was the closest thing to a famous passenger they had that day, so the front of the *Evening Standard* used a picture of me to illustrate the story. I assume people glancing at the paper thought I was dead.

Feeling very much alive, I eventually got to New York and met up with Carrie. Of course we thought the whole idea of going to this wedding was hysterical, but we were also undeniably excited. We got to the church with time to spare and found some seats. We opted for the balcony where we could get a good, uninterrupted view of the who's who of show business that had shown up.

Liza has connections going back to her mother's time in Hollywood right up to Studio 54 and beyond, while David came from the world of pop music. Lauren Bacall, David Hasselhoff, Michael Douglas, Elaine Paige . . . the guest list could best be described as eclectic. The headline acts were Elizabeth Taylor as matron of honour and Michael Jackson as best man. The whole thing was like one of those Agatha Christie movies where they just round up as many famous people as possible and start filming.

The ceremony itself was slightly delayed, not because we were waiting for a nervous bride, but because Elizabeth Taylor had got cold feet. In fact, she had literally got cold feet, because she had forgotten her shoes. It seems an odd oversight but, nonetheless, a car had to be dispatched to her hotel in order to complete her outfit. Whitney Houston was one of the very few no-shows, so Natalie Cole stepped in to serenade the couple down the aisle.

When the minister declared that they were man and wife, David lunged at Liza and proceeded to kiss her like a man who had

149

decided to eat a whole trout headfirst. It was an image that, once seen, was never forgotten. They produced such staggering amounts of saliva I'm surprised the front few pews weren't handed those plastic ponchos you get on a log-flume ride.

Over a thousand people had been invited to the reception, which was held downtown near Wall Street. We stood patiently outside while everyone was checked in. Just before we reached the door, a small woman pushed past us, apologising in a familiar rasp. It was Carol Channing. Mia Farrow and her son, Satchel (now Ronan), stood and chatted while Rosie O'Donnell glared at me like I was a waiter who had forgotten to bring out a tray of drinks. Our table consisted of all the British guests and, perhaps because there were so many people there who had been in rehab, I feel our little table got more than its fair share of drinks. I'm guessing I must have been quite drunk in order to think it was a good idea to apologise to Mel C for all the lesbian jokes I had made about her.

Apparently there is never a good time for that.

Meanwhile, the best man, Michael Jackson, ate his meal alone, his table surrounded by a ring of security men. Being the king of pop did not look like a great deal of fun.

After the meal it was time for the speeches and entertainment. The best man made his way to the stage. I'm not sure if Michael Jackson had bought one of those books on how to make a successful best man's speech, but if he had, he never read beyond the advice to keep it brief. He barely uttered the names of the happy couple before he scuttled off to look for his other glove. A large orchestra then began to play for an endless array of acts, from The Doobie Brothers to Brian May. In truth I didn't recognise many of them. *OK!* magazine had bought the rights and I insisted on having my picture taken with Helena Christensen: I knew they would use her photo, and I wanted some sort of proof that I was there.

In the papers the next day, Mickey Rooney declared it to have been the best wedding he had ever attended. Given that he had been to at least nine where he had been the groom, I think we can trust his opinion.

★   ★   ★

When the news of their split came fourteen months later, nobody was particularly shocked, but I still remember that on that spring day in 2002 Liza looked truly blissfully happy. Whatever the emotional and financial cost of the marriage, who can say where Liza would be now if David hadn't brought her back into the limelight? The divorce brought with it allegations and counter-claims about violence and financial skulduggery, which just added to the bizarre vision we all had of this marriage.

After various attempts to desperately cling on to his newfound celebrity status David has finally drifted back to the world of producing, but what about Liza Minnelli?

I've seen her several times since the wedding — usually backstage at one of her shows, or on stage at one of mine. The rawness remains and I feel very fond and protective of her. The impulse is to try and help her in some way but I'm not sure anyone can. She is unique and that somehow means that she will always be alone, no matter how much love surrounds her. The daughter of Judy Garland who grew up to be a huge star herself has to exist in a bubble. Her experience combined with her talent mean that she is for ever cut off from the rest of the human race. Her voice may not be what it was and her behaviour can be somewhat erratic, but that is no longer why people sit enthralled or stand to applaud.

A couple of years ago she was performing a version of the song 'I Must Have That Man' on my chat show, her dark, oil-slick eyes connecting with the camera like she was staring at her lover across a pillow. As we watched the rehearsal on the monitor, it wasn't the most beautiful thing to hear, and some of the team began to groan. I stopped them. 'No matter what, that woman performing on our show tonight is Liza Minnelli and that means something.'

It has been an extreme privilege for me to spend time with her and in some small ways to actually work with her. I can't claim to call her an old chum but her life has been the biggest, most brilliant cabaret of all. The vortex of need is also a bottomless well. She may well be the last of her kind and we must treasure her.

★　★　★

Dolly! Just to hear her name is to be happy. Truthfully she doesn't really belong in a chapter about divas because although she is an icon there is nothing tortured or troubled about her. She revels in her persona, her fans and her music. I'm sure she has an 'Off' button but she has no interest in pressing it when anyone else is around. She is pure joy, and that is what she wants to share.

I had always been aware of her when I was growing up. Country music is hugely popular in Ireland and there can't be a child alive that wouldn't be drawn to the bright candy colours and enormous breasts of Dolly Parton. I had laughed at her jokes on countless talk shows and loved her in the movie *9 to 5*, but she wasn't really one of my obsessions.

Scott changed all that. My second serious boyfriend was besotted by Dolly. At Christmas, out would come her festive album, *A Very Dolly Christmas*, and no road trip was complete without a stack of her CDs. With all the over-the-top outfits and well-rehearsed self-deprecating quips, it's easy to forget that Dolly Parton is an extraordinarily talented songwriter, musician and performer.

Nowadays the guest list for my shows is made up of the biggest stars that are on the promotional circuit — we are very much a mainstream programme made for a broad BBC One audience. Back in our early Channel 4 incarnation I was like some camp emperor pointing at pictures in magazines: 'Bring me that one!' I even got them to fly in Michael Learned, who had played the mother in *The Waltons*; Wonder Woman herself, Lynda Carter, was washed and brought to my studio; and someone was dispatched to get me Miles O'Keeffe, who played Tarzan opposite Bo Derek's Jane. Like an eccentric millionaire I chose guests based on whom I'd like to meet. Happily my tastes seemed to chime with the audience's.

Dolly Parton would be a dream guest on the show and might also help cheer up my boyfriend.

I'm not sure how it all happened, but I got the call to say that Ms Parton was in town, that she would like to meet me and, based on how that went, she might agree to do the show.

I puckered my lips in preparation for a great deal of ass kissing, and headed off to her hotel.

Unlike most major stars, Dolly wasn't staying in one of the handful of well-known luxury hotels — she had chosen one slightly off the beaten track, but equally lovely. Why? Because it was cheaper, and she got the biggest suite in London. Don't ever try accusing Dolly of being a fool.

I was led through double doors into a sitting room. Nice, but then I had seen hotel suites before. Then I was led through some more doors into a large library. That I had not seen before. Through more doors I could see a staircase leading to an upper level. This wasn't a hotel room, it was a house with complimentary shower caps and slippers. I sat taking in all the trappings of being a superstar and then, in the distance, I heard singing. Like a scene from a fabulous movie that I had no right to be in, more doors burst open and there she was dancing towards me, her wide, red-lipped mouth smiling and singing, 'He's Going to Marry Me'! It was the song she ended up singing on our show.

The meeting was odd in that Dolly didn't seem to have any questions about the show and was only interested in being lovely to me and making me laugh. Had she got confused? Was her next appointment with a super fan that had some sort of terminal disease? I loved every second of it but didn't really see the point of it. I guess it must have served some kind of purpose, however, because it was confirmed that Ms Parton would be joining us on set.

At the time we didn't have music on the show — it just ended with a game or stunt of some sort. It wasn't until we went to five nights a week that we finally built a performance area and invested in a few more flashing lights. In order to get Dolly on the show we made an exception. The show would open with her bursting from a wedding cake to perform her song about getting married and then we would record the show as normal. It is such a happy memory, sitting at my desk with the actual Dolly Parton singing live just ten feet away. The chat was effortless, of course — when the guest is as good as Dolly, you are left with the feeling that there was a real connection. She made me feel like her friend.

It sounds like such an over-the-top, saccharine thing to say, but to meet her is to fall in love with her. Dolly is such a huge star but she engages with you in an incredibly genuine way. There is no sense that she's just there to sell a record or tickets. She is having the time of her life and really likes you. When I introduced her to Scott she was exactly the same to him. His love deepened and I got the prize for being the Best Boyfriend Ever. I don't even think it's a showbiz trick or a social skill. In the moment, it is 100 per cent true. She is like a white witch with a stunning selection of wigs.

My sweet delusion was deepened further when we were contacted about making a special show with her. The idea was we would visit her personal theme park in Pigeon Forge, Tennessee, and explore the area together while she would perform a few songs. We pitched the idea to Channel 4 and they liked it. Needless to say I loved the proposal, and everyone signed off on it. *Graham Goes to Dollywood* would be an hour-long special to be aired at Christmas. For me, the whole thing was Christmas come early.

We decided that the best time to film it would be at the end of the summer before we started production of the next series. Plans were made. Graham Stuart and I flew out to LA to meet Dolly to discuss some of the content. We needed to know how much access we would have and also not plan any elaborate shoots that she wasn't happy with. Oddly, one of my favourite sequences in the film was Dolly's suggestion. The two of us were going to duet on 'Islands in the Stream'. So far, so awful. What we didn't know was that next door to Dollywood, she had recently opened a water park called Dolly Splash Country. The business-minded Dolly had seen an opportunity for promotion and explained how funny it would be if we sang it floating through the park in rubber rings.

She was right — it was an hilarious concept. The only down side was that we would actually have to do it.

I'm very good at forgetting about the next job until I've finished the one I'm doing so all thoughts of our film left my head while we taped more episodes and went on to make another documentary for Channel 4. This one was called *Si Graham Norton* and involved me staying with a family in Mexico City. Then, just before heading to Pigeon Forge, I had agreed to record a week's worth of radio shows in New York, so while the rest of the crew were in Tennessee getting ready I wouldn't fly into Knoxville, the nearest airport, until the Monday.

Monday, 10 September 2001.

We were commissioned to make a frothy Christmas show full of Dolly but there was probably a more interesting film to be made about the making of the show.

Pigeon Forge is dry, which is to say you cannot buy alcohol in it. I knew this and was almost looking forward to being abstemious. It would be good for me and I might lose some weight. The crew had other ideas. Part of their preparations had involved driving to the nearest town that did have booze and stocking up. This meant that what I had imagined being a clear-headed early first night turned into a wine-fuelled reunion. I don't know what time I stumbled to bed but I know I looked at my alarm clock with a sense of dread.

157

The next day I turned on my usual morning TV show, *Live! with Regis and Kelly*. It's like a radio show but filmed and, like the rest of America, I mostly tuned in because I enjoyed the company of the hosts. It wasn't on. At first I thought that maybe Tennessee didn't get the show but then I worked out that the news was coming from New York and it had been extended. Moving between the bathroom and my bed I figured out that some sort of light aircraft had hit the side of a building, and it seemed like a pretty small story to be delaying the start of Regis and Kelly for. I got in the lift, my mind busy with thoughts of getting a coffee. Down in the lobby a few people were gathered around the TV. A second plane had flown into another tower. My fuzzy brain began to clear. This wasn't an accident. It was a co-ordinated attack and now I was watching the action replays and realising the scale of the buildings and the planes and the seriousness of it. A sense of dread and fear descended on our group.

We found ourselves whispering for no reason as we loaded our van and made our way to Dollywood. The park is always closed on a Tuesday at that time of year so we had the place to ourselves. We weren't due to film with Dolly herself until the next day. We walked through the deserted fake streets of the theme park towards our first location. The whole place had the eerie atmosphere of a zombie movie and, to make it worse, all the speakers which normally blared out endless hours of Dolly classics had been retuned to a news radio station. We heard snippets as we walked: ' . . . state of emergency . . . loss of life'.

We spent the morning filming a sequence about finding some pubic hair in Dolly's bed. The show must go on.

At lunch a local man brought us some sandwiches and cold drinks.

'Any more news from New York?' we asked.

'Oh, I think some tower fell down,' he replied, as he got into his golf buggy and drove off.

The man was clearly an idiot. In order to get better information we walked down a track till we found a fake plastic rock that doubled as a speaker. We huddled around it sitting on the ground and listened slack-jawed to the announcer. The twin towers had collapsed. Two more planes were down. The Pentagon had been hit. Where was this going to end? Was this how we would learn of the end of the world?

That night we had been due to film at Dolly's Dixie Stampede, a sort of dinner theatre extravaganza involving horse riding and stunts. The arena holds 2,000 people. We just assumed that that night's performance would be cancelled. Word reached us — no, it was going ahead as planned. We were still all in shock at what was going on but slowly it was becoming clear that we felt more of a connection to New York than most of the people we were meeting. We asked one man if he was worried about anyone in Manhattan. 'No. I had a cousin that went there once, but no.' The USA is bigger and more disparate than any nation I know. When they listened to the news on the speakers, it was like us hearing about a train derailment in China. It was foreign news; it was a world they couldn't relate to.

We arrived at the venue that night astonished to find it packed to the rafters. The show itself is very hard to describe but it sort of follows the pattern of your meal. Clowns chase chickens around the arena while you are served chicken. Races are held with pigs while the staff dish out piles of pork chops — I imagine the smell in the air really motivates those piggies to run faster. I looked around at the crowd cheering and waving flags. Didn't they know their president was hiding in a bunker? The evening ended with the riders of the south and the north coming together as the United States, and a rousing rendition of the national anthem while an enormous Stars and Stripes was unfurled from the ceiling. It seemed incredibly charged with emotion and we were all left in tears, but at the back of my mind I was thinking, 'Maybe it's always like this?' What moved me most was the blind faith of this crowd. They had absolute belief in their god, president and country, and the bloodiest, most horrific of days would not change that.

The park opened the next day as normal and the happy, relaxed crowds roared with delight every time they caught a glimpse of Dolly Parton. Following the attacks, it seemed all mobile phone signals had been switched off for security reasons. Long-distance lines were constantly engaged. It was a huge relief when our phones finally started working and I managed to get hold of my mother to let her know I was all right.

'What's that noise in the background?' she wanted to know.

'That's a carousel,' I replied, explaining that the rides were all operating as normal.

'For God's sake, and I'm here in Ireland. It's a national day of mourning. I can't even get a pint of milk.'

Worlds apart in all sorts of ways.

Though the small town of Pigeon Forge seemed blissfully unconcerned, large parts of America had shut down, and so had air travel. This gave us a forced calmness. Had we been able to, we might have been tempted to flee home after the attacks but because we couldn't, we just settled down to make our silly film, complete with fake snow and elf costumes.

No matter how little needs to get done, filming is a very long process and necessitates lots of waiting around. I felt like I had passed another test when Dolly's Winnebago door swung open and I was invited in.

Even though we were sitting in her own personal theme park in a part of America where she provides a huge amount of employment, she treated me like an equal. We were just two people working together. I don't want to betray any trust she might have placed in me as she chatted without a filter but I don't think she'll mind me passing on these few nuggets. Dolly is very proud of her tiny waist and is keen to show it off, so she doesn't want it padded out by the battery pack for her personal microphone. For this reason she has a special battery-pack holder built into all of her wigs.

Not only must this be incredibly uncomfortable, but large slices of her brain must have been cooked by all the microwaves so close to her head. Still, her waistline is very petite. She talked about her husband and the road trips they like to take. Some big sunglasses and no wigs mean she is pretty much anonymous as she travels through the towns and villages where she is worshipped. One woman I met in New York who was from Tennessee asked me where I was headed next and I explained about our little film with Dolly. Her eyes filled with tears and she said, 'That woman has done more for our state than any governor ever has.'

Lots of stars don't forget their roots, but I doubt there are many that continue to tend and feed them in the way Dolly Parton does. Every child in the region gets a free book every month from birth until the age of five. She told me there are children who only know her as 'the book lady', unaware of her coat of many colours or 'Jolene'. Added to this, financial incentives were put in place to encourage students to finish high school, while local hospitals and universities all owe her an enormous thank you. Dolly is always first to poke fun at herself but to the people of Tennessee, she is no laughing matter.

One of the last things we filmed was our water-based extravaganza. All through our trip, whenever we explained the sequence, people invariably responded, 'And Dolly has agreed to this?' Even on the morning setting up, we were aware of a great deal of incredulity.

'Miss Dolly does not like water.'

'She'll never get wet!'

Given that I was worried about how stupid I was going to look bobbing along in a rubber ring, I did wonder if Dolly might think better of the whole idea.

Apparently selling tickets to Dolly Splash Country was more important than her dignity because soon her vehicle pulled up. The door opened and out stepped Dolly ready for her close-up. She was dressed in what I assume was a custom-made wetsuit, which showed off every hard-earned curve. On her head sat a special wet-look wig and on her feet were a pair of her trademark high-heeled mules. She teetered to the water's edge where her rubber ring awaited. The moment of truth. She stepped out of her shoes to take the plunge. I noticed two things. Firstly she was still wearing stockings under the wetsuit and secondly her heels, even without the shoes, didn't touch the ground. A lifetime of impossibly high heels had left her hamstrings so short that putting her feet flat on the ground would have resulted in her falling over like a badly erected Christmas tree.

Throughout the repeated playbacks of the song and time spent being shoved around in the water, Dolly never once complained. And yet she still managed to communicate very firmly when she had had enough. It was a wrap.

When I was invited on to *Desert Island Discs* in 2004 I was immodest enough to bring my duet with Dolly. But I thought if I really was on a desert island, then listening to that recording would be one of the few things to make me smile.

* * *

I don't know how celebrities make friends with each other. I have seen guests after the show exchanging numbers but somehow I never have the nerve or the inclination. If I did get the number, what then? I'd have to call them and then we'd have to see each other and then I'd have to talk to them and then we'd probably have to do it again. My social life seems pretty full with people I adore, so the idea of hanging out with people who can't just socialise with your regular friends in your usual haunts seems exhausting. Having said all that, I did feel close to Dolly at the end of our time together, especially given the extraordinary backdrop of world events we had shared. However, no numbers or emails were exchanged and we simply went back to our lives.

Probably a couple of years had passed when I got an invitation to go and see Dolly Parton perform at Wembley. Before I could reply there was a second call. Would Graham like to say hi to Dolly before the concert? I was thrilled. It appeared she did remember me! I excitedly said yes.

It's unusual to see performers before a show but I thought she must want to shoot off straight afterwards, be it to bed or the next venue. Everyone has a different way of doing things.

On the night of the show I arrived quite early and the doors weren't open yet. I knocked forlornly on the glass but no security guard was willing to take pity on me. I stood like a slightly sweaty waxwork while hordes of Dolly fans had their picture taken with me. Suddenly I heard a cry of 'Graham!' which sounded familiar. I turned to find the fabulous actress Miriam Margolyes by my side. Hurrah! If you aren't familiar with Miriam, shame on you. She isn't very tall and appears to be square-shaped. A mop of wiry grey curls sits on top of a face that is usually all smiles, with eyes that shine like naughty marbles. It turned out that she too had been invited to say hello to the great Ms Parton before the show. We clung to each other and waited.

When the doors opened a nice man approached us and gave us some stickers that said something on them about meet and greet. We were then told where to stand and that someone would be along to collect us shortly. As we loitered I noticed a few other people wearing the same sticker as us. Dolly certainly knew a lot of people in London. Another door opened and we were ushered inside with what now seemed to be a very large group of people. Everyone settled into an orderly queue snaking along a backstage corridor. Something didn't feel quite right. Miriam turned to the people ahead of us in the line.

'How do you know Ms Parton?'

'We don't. My husband bought us the meet and greet tickets.'

I think it is fair to say that Miriam and I lost some of the spring in our step. It seemed we were waiting to meet our good friend Dolly along with many others who had paid for the privilege. Everyone else just wanted a picture with her before they went into the auditorium. This was going to be wildly embarrassing. Either she wouldn't remember us and we'd be humiliated or she would know who we were and wonder what on earth we were doing paying to have a photo taken with her. This was not the reunion I had been hoping for.

People react to situations in different ways: I stood, head bowed, hoping for the concrete floor to open up and swallow me whole; Miriam, on the other hand, suddenly braced herself, arms in the air and legs planted wide apart. In her booming, theatrical voice she announced, 'Pause for fart!' Before anyone could react she let rip with a low, rumbling roar that seemed as loud as any thunder ever heard in the Blue Ridge Mountains. It seemed the Dolly fans were getting a lot more than they'd paid for that night.

I assumed everyone would burst into howls of laughter but instead we just heard a few sniggers and watched as people turned away. I blame their nerves at the prospect of meeting their idol.

166

Eventually we reached a large black drape and it was obvious that on the other side of it was Dolly Parton. In the event, it wasn't nearly as awkward as I'd feared. Dolly did recognise me and was completely lovely but seemed to find it perfectly natural that I had chosen to stand and wait for my picture. We posed and then I was ushered out. It reminded me of when I was a child and we had queued up to see Santa Claus, except there wasn't a depressed reindeer standing in a wire pen in the corner of the room. Just the scent of one, thanks to Miriam.

I never got my copy of that backstage photograph but did spend a fabulous couple of hours listening to Dolly sing. Since then I've been to a few more concerts and would obviously love to have her back on the show. And please don't think I'm complaining about what happened with Dolly — I'm simply trying to illustrate how special she is. I have spent just as much time with many other people, including the camera crew and production team when we worked together, and I don't wonder why we don't hang out. That's because I didn't fall in love with them. Dolly casts a spell stronger than even she is aware of. I have no interest in the whole idea of famous friends, but the warmth and love that pour from Dolly Parton mean that even if she were a waitress in a diner or a dog walker, people would still be drawn to her. So much of her is a frothy façade — the high hair, the pink nails, the giant bosoms, but behind it all is a brain the size of a planet and a heart that beats for the world. I love you, Dolly Parton!

★ ★ ★

Stars are curious creatures. They all have talent but so do thousands of other people we have never heard of. Over the years, it has been proven that with the right marketing and production, those people can be plucked from obscurity and for a few years burn as bright as any other star, but I defy anyone to explain why some people last the course and become divas and legends. Yes, they are driven in a way we will never understand. Yes, they seem to need it more than other people. Yes, the public seems hard-wired to their hearts, but there is always something else. A diva isn't just a rude bitch that had a couple of disco hits in the early eighties. The older I get the more it seems to me that the handful of true divas weren't created, they were born.

Viva la diva!

5

Booze

The eerie science-fiction wailing of my phone's alarm wakes me. The shadows on the ceiling tell me that it's light outside. The dogs look at me warily. Is this really it? Are we going out for a walk? Even before I heave my sagging carcass out of bed I know that something isn't quite right. Am I late for something? Did I forget to . . . ? And then it comes to me. My feet! I was supposed to get a pedicure before today and now it's too late.

I stumble into the bathroom to look for a few basic tools and then start hacking at and sanding my dry, calloused hooves.

Normally, I don't bother very much about what lurks inside my socks. It is very rare for anyone to see my feet and if they do, they are either a member of the medical profession, and so I assume they have seen worse things, or they are someone whom I'm encouraging to give their full attention to other parts of my anatomy.

Today, however, was different because this was the day when I was going to be filmed treading grapes for my very own wine.

I have long been an admirer of wines from New Zealand, especially sauvignon blancs from the Marlborough region thanks for asking. I

169

must have mentioned this in some interview or other because the television production team was approached by a vineyard called Invivo to see if we'd like them to supply some bottles for our guests in the green room. Like any sane person being offered free booze, we said yes. It turned out it wasn't just very affordable, it was also delicious. In return they were able to tell people that various *bona fide* celebrities, plus me, drank their product.

They must have done a good job because I walked into an off-licence once and the man behind the counter hardly looked up before he pointed and barked: 'It's over there.'

I was a little thrown. Did he think I was someone else? Was he expecting me to fix one of his fridges? 'Sorry. What's over there?'

He just about managed to stop himself from rolling his eyes at my stupidity. 'Your wine. The Invivo.'

I felt obliged to buy some, and once I'd done that it seemed silly not to drink it as well. I'd only gone in for chewing gum.

Having sold this one extra bottle, the guys at Invivo obviously saw the huge marketing potential of using my name and asked if they could bottle some sauvignon blanc especially for me, with a personalised label. Given the amount of the stuff I neck, the only surprise was that no one had offered to do this before.

The plan was that they would pack some grapes in a cool box, fly to London, get me to stamp on them and then fly the juice back to the vineyard to make up my own private batch. They would film the whole journey and use it for PR.

Looking at the state of my feet that morning, I felt the only publicity their promotional film might get would be in some fetish magazine for lovers of dry skin. It is still being fermented as I write so I've yet to taste any of it. I genuinely worry that it may have a slight taste of foot lotion because of the copious amount of moisturising I did on the day.

Up until the moment of actually stamping I was more concerned with my feet than the grapes. This was because I sort of assumed it was all going to be faked. The winemaker man, Tim Lightbourne, who set up Invivo with his business partner, Rob Cameron, wouldn't have actually travelled over 11,000 miles with a box of grapes. Obviously you would just pop into Waitrose, buy a couple of bunches, take the pictures and then throw the murky juice away before heading home. Sadly, the winemakers from the land of the Hobbit are far more principled than that. Matters didn't improve when I discovered that Tim, far from being the red-nosed burly yokel I had been expecting, turned out to be young, buff and ridiculously handsome. Normally I love meeting attractive young men, but somehow standing in a bucket of grapes, devoid of shoes and socks, with my jeans yanked past my chunky calves, I wasn't feeling my best.

There is a time and a place for encountering beauty.

★ ★ ★

It reminded me of when I was having a routine series of health check-ups around the time of my fiftieth birthday. I found myself sitting on a hospital trolley wearing the dreaded backless gown and some very odd ankle socks with textured soles. The nurse kept telling me the doctor would be along in a minute to explain the procedure. After a few minutes the curtain was drawn back and a man stepped into the cubicle. I expected harp music to play and some small bluebirds to start flying around his head. Young and blond, he looked like he should be appearing as a doctor in some glossy American soap opera, not in an actual hospital with germs and pale green linoleum. He was far from the usual breed of balding, pot-bellied specialists that I had been dealing with up until then.

He smiled a perfect, gleaming smile and told me in great detail about how he was going to perform my colonoscopy. I know women sometimes have affairs with their gynaecologist but I'm fairly sure there isn't a colonoscopy doctor on earth who has started dating a patient. As he began to put on his rubber gloves, most of my brain was covered with a blanket of embarrassment, but a small corner of it found time to wonder what possessed this beautiful man to focus on this particular field of medicine as his speciality. I rolled onto my side acutely aware that he was not going to be seeing me at my best.

In better news, my colon was as clean as a whistle.

Tim the wine man took great care with the grey-green liquid that I had managed to extract from his grapes. (I am aware of how wrong that sentence sounds but I assure you, that is what happened.) The precious bottle was put in his bag and off he went. I presume some customs officer noticed that it contained more than 100ml and promptly confiscated it. I guarantee the quality of the wine will not suffer in the slightest.

I haven't always been a wine drinker. Obviously there was a time in my life when I was a child and whatever you may imagine being raised in Ireland was like, I never suckled Guinness or whiskey from a baby's bottle. Although my father worked for a brewery, there wasn't much booze in the house growing up. My mother wasn't very keen and my father, while visiting dozens of pubs every day, had seen just how destructive drinking could be. If we had visitors, tumblers of gin and tonic might be handed around but even they were fairly exotic. More likely that the ladies would sip a sherry while the men tackled whiskey. When it came to ice cubes, well, guests were as likely to find a piece of moon rock in their drink. Dinner parties were a rare event but on the odd occasion that my parents held a *soirée* for neighbours such as the Nicholsons or the Skuses, then wine would be served. As far as I'm aware, when I was a boy in Ireland there were only three varieties of wine: Blue Nun, the one with the nuns on the label; Black Tower, the tall one with a short neck; and Mateus Rosé, the one that looked lovely as a lamp when it was covered with shells.

Because of my father's job, all the glasses, tea towels and ashtrays in the house were branded with the various logos of the drinks he represented. Guinness, Harp Lager and Smithwick's were the main ones, but Guinness seemed to have the lion's share of the merchandising. I never tired of being given a bottle of Coke in a glass with the famous harp logo and pretending that I was drinking in a pub.

Of course, when it came to any encounters with the real thing, like everyone else having their first tentative sips, I just wasn't very keen on the taste. I'm sure some schools in the seventies were full of hard drinkers but ours didn't seem to be. Occasionally we would buy cans of shandy, but even that tasted too strong. The first alcoholic drink that I remember being able to pretend to like was Bacardi and Coke. Sometimes as I got older I would go out with my father and I felt incredibly grown up with my signature cocktail. If I drank one now I think I might be sick.

It wasn't until I reached university in Cork that I began to get into my booze groove. I'm not sure how it happened but I began to actually enjoy pints of lager. I remember many occasions when we were drunk but because of our extreme poverty as students, I can't imagine that we actually drank very much. There was an unending search for the cheapest possible bottle of wine. Does anyone else remember Boone's Farm? It had the word 'wine' on the label though I doubt very much a single grape was harmed in its manufacture. It came in various flavours but it didn't take a student of the sciences to figure out that Strawberry Hill had the highest alcohol content. If you've never encountered this bargain beverage, suffice to say it is sweeter than the average drink. It tastes like it has more sugar in it than a bag of sugar. We loved it.

A lot of our drinking was done in our various student digs. Some people still lived at home while others clubbed together to rent houses in the suburbs. I've always been a very social creature but when it comes to domestic arrangements I tend to enjoy my isolation, so I

175

became a fan of the bedsit or, to be more precise, the very cheap bedsit. When I tell you that thirty years later, every single one I lived in has been demolished, you will get some idea of their quality.

Washington Street in the centre of Cork must have been affluent at one stage with the courthouse and terraces of tall Georgian buildings, and it is again, with a cluster of the city's most popular bars and restaurants, but in the early eighties, all it could boast was a fish and chip shop, an ice cream parlour, a discount carpet shop and, at the end closest to the university, a small wine bar and restaurant called Café Lorca.

The first bedsit I got was at the very top of one of the tall, red-brick buildings. It was a narrow room that ran the depth of the building, so I had a dormer window at the front and the back. From one you could look out at a tangle of television aerials and endless grey slate roofs that always seemed to meet an equally grey sky; the other window faced the opposite side of Washington Street and just looked into another building of flats. Like looking into a seedy doll's house, I got to know my various neighbours as I peered at them undetected from my darkened lair: the couple that fought, the woman who never stopped brushing her hair and, of course, the compulsive wanker. I shared a toilet with the bedsit tucked beside mine in the eaves but luckily no one ever lived there while I was in residence.

Every week a hunched man with greasy hair

came to collect the rent. He looked like a farmer but his student tenants were his only unhappy crop. Having just read Dostoyevsky's *Crime and Punishment*, I fantasised about killing him and dumping his body out of the window into the bin-filled alley below. How long would he lie undiscovered? Could anyone ever figure out that I was the murderer? These were dark days fuelled by a self-indulgent teenage angst. After initially thinking that I had found my tribe I had slowly started to feel once more like an outsider. The boy that didn't fit in. I remember I collected the bodies of the large heavy flies who always seemed to be throwing their lazy black bodies against the dirty panes of glass no matter what the weather was like outside. I was not at my happiest.

Slowly I noticed fewer and fewer people coming and going on the stairs until eventually it appeared I was the last resident in the whole building. I'd wanted to live alone and now I truly was. I remember lying in my little attic cell listening to the sounds of drunken couples breaking through the front door of the building so they could have sex in the stairwell. The greasy-haired farmer told me I would have to move out. One might have assumed that this news would have made me punch the air with joy, but no — I didn't want to leave or, more to the point, I could not be bothered to move.

Eventually, the farmer grew tired of waiting and found me a bedsit in another one of his buildings further down the street. This one was above the ice cream parlour and other people, including a friend of mine from university, John Fitzgerald, actually lived there. Clearly this was going to be a big move up in the world of student accommodation.

The week I was moving out of my first bedsit I found a large dead rat on the stairs. I was horrified on two counts — firstly, I had been living in a building with rats, and secondly, it appeared that rats could climb stairs. It made the prospect of moving seem a little easier.

★ ★ ★

Remembering my days and nights as a student in Cork makes me glad not to have children of my own. We were that terrifying combination of reckless, fearless and clueless. I'm sure young people are exactly the same today, and they have so many more temptations and pressures than we did thirty years ago. Of course everyone encounters alcohol when they leave home, but not everyone turns into the massive boozehound I did.

What was it about drinking that I liked so much? For me it has always been a social thing — yes, I might have a glass of wine when sitting alone with the TV and the dogs, but I enjoy it so much more when doing it with others. Back in 1981, I was eighteen years old and I had never had the sensation of truly fitting in. Drink helped. It created a level playing-field because after a few glasses we all felt the same. It made us laugh more, it made me funnier, it gave the group its glue. Even now when I walk into some showbiz bash, I feel that teenage fear and insecurity. Where's the waiter with the tray? Found him . . . and let the small talk begin!

I've been very lucky in that I've never hung out with people where alcohol unleashes their violence or tears. Obviously I've witnessed that side of drinking but I avoid it at all costs. A few years ago a group of people from my drama school were at my house for Christmas drinks and one of the women, after too many flutes of champagne, started to cry. As far as we could tell she wasn't actually upset about anything, she was merely being the worst possible version of a drunk actress. I remember she ended up lying on the floor sobbing and wailing, while we ignored her. Bailey, however, sauntered casually into the room and assessed the situation. I'm not sure if he thought it might cheer the woman up, but he walked over and started trying to hump her. I may never have laughed more.

When you're getting to know each other in the beginning booze can be a strange new friend and there are many lessons along the way. Even now at fifty-one I find myself out with friends who still haven't learnt the most basic of rules — eat something! An Irish woman I met in West Cork put it best when she referred to our entire, beautifully cooked meal as 'soakage'. It's about priorities.

Most other teething problems seem to simply fade away. I no longer get the dreaded 'wheelies', that sensation that the whole room is spinning. On numerous occasions as a student I found myself lying on bedsit floors while in my head I appeared to be on a transatlantic yacht. Normally I felt this was nature's way of telling me it was time for bed. The other side effect, which is much harder to shake, is the tendency to vomit. We all did it and with various degrees of success. I expect my fellow revellers might have contradictory memories but I'm pretty sure I normally managed to get to the toilet in time. By the way, that's the toilet, never the sink. It always baffles me when people do that in a sink, but then I suppose they are making decisions with a very drunk brain. No one plans to be sick, which is why it can take anyone by surprise. About ten years ago after quite a big night in Manchester, myself and a good friend ended up with a random group of people heading back to someone's flat. It was nicely decorated in a variety of shades of beige and oatmeal. We were sitting on the matching sofas chatting about our night. It was in no way raucous. My friend suddenly stood up as if he'd just remembered he'd left the gas on and then, with no warning, opened his mouth to release a gushing torrent of stomach contents. It was as close to satanic possession as anything I have ever witnessed. The girl in *The Exorcist* was just a little car sick in comparison. We made our excuses and headed home, leaving the world just a little less beige.

Sometimes a night just takes more twists and turns than you expect and all your good intentions end up in the gutter, along with your keys, mobile phone and dignity. After I had moved to London I came back to visit my parents but of course also wanted to hang out with my friends in Cork city. I caught the bus to travel the twenty miles or so from Bandon (no smoke) to Cork (the big smoke). I had arranged to meet a few friends in the Long Valley on Winthrop Street, my favourite pub in the city. When I was a student I always thought the name referred to its very long urinal but in later years I was told it was just a name, or might refer to the original length of the room which had stretched in a dog-leg to re-emerge around the corner on Oliver Plunkett Street.

Mrs Moynihan and her husband, Humphrey, ran the place with a mixture of iron fists and eccentric whimsy. Mrs Moynihan had no Christian name and her womanly charms were for ever hidden underneath a white cotton coat, the sort favoured by butchers and doctors. A thick thatch of hair framed a face of what could only be described as nervous features: her thin lips twitched, and looking you in the eye seemed to physically pain her. The husband Humphrey was smaller and thinner than his wife. His long, sad face was only remarkable for one thing: he had a moustache as close to what might be called a 'Hitler' as I had ever seen in real life. In between serving pints and barking prices at penny-counting students, he played old records on the ancient gramophone he kept perched on the bar. The music tended to be a selection of light operettas and a great many German marching songs. We didn't ask.

For hours they stood behind the bar pulling pints and making the most delicious sandwiches I've ever tasted: thick slices of fresh white bread

181

holding roast meat and salads dripping with mayonnaise. I usually couldn't afford one but when I did have the money I always hoped it would be Mrs Moynihan who made it. She was not what you would describe as warm or a barrel of laughs but I'm sure she knew just by glancing at me that this would be the only fresh food I would be having for days and sliced the meat accordingly.

Sadly, on this occasion, I only placed an order for drinks. I was planning to head back to Bandon fairly early, but the plan started to go wrong as more people I knew showed up and then suggested we head on to another bar to see various people I had been at college with. In between rounds of drinks I did mention that we should eat something but by the time we staggered into a restaurant the kitchen was shut. Oh well. We switched to red wine and ordered a slice of cheesecake each. Delicious.

Suddenly I realised that if I didn't move fairly quickly I might miss the last bus back to Bandon. I hastily made my farewells and ran for the bus station. I must have been making good time because I decided to make a pit stop at McDonald's in order to have something for the road. Clutching my little sack of fat and salt I stumbled up the steps of the bus just in time. I found a seat and wolfed down my burger and chips, too drunk to care what the few other passengers thought.

The journey takes about an hour and that night I was very aware that not only did this particular bus not seem to have very good suspension but that the road surface itself was incredibly bumpy. I'm not sure where all that money from the EU was going but none of it seemed to have been allocated to filling potholes on the main Cork to Bandon road. Normally quite a robust traveller, I was becoming rather concerned by how queasy I was feeling. My mouth filled with the tell-tale saliva and I realised that I was going to be sick. Happily, I still had my McDonald's bag so in as discreet a manner as I could manage, I allowed the rich mix of things that had been in my stomach to make a hasty exit. In a fairly sloppy version of recycling, the bag was full once more. I hadn't even started to come up with a plan for disposing of the bag when the bottom of it split. Empty again. This bag was having a very busy night.

For the rest of the journey I just sat there willing us to arrive. Finally, the orange glow of street lighting announced we had reached our destination. I got up and fled the scene of the crime.

Very sweetly, my dad had suggested he come and collect me from the bus and drive me home. I did my best to try and sound sober, moving slowly and deliberately through sentences, pronouncing every syllable, desperate not to slur. I imagine to the sober ear it sounded like I had suffered a stroke and was learning to speak again. Back at home, I discovered that Mr and Mrs Nicholson had popped in from next door for a drink and I was just in time for supper.

This was a strange ritual that seems to have

died out now, where, just before bed, my mother wheeled in a trolley with tea, sandwiches and various cakes and biscuits. I really do think the famine has given the Irish a fear of starving to death in our sleep.

The Nicholsons feigned delight to see me and asked questions about how I was getting on in London and I politely replied, sipping my tea with all the delicacy of Maggie Smith in *Downton Abbey*. I suppose we chatted for about half an hour before they made their excuses and headed home. I kissed Mum and Dad goodnight and headed to my bedroom. I felt a quiet pride because, against all the odds, I had managed not to embarrass myself or my parents. This night was ending well.

Very ready for bed I sat down and bent over to untie my shoes. They were covered in vomit. I thought back to what had just occurred: the car journey with my father; the tea and chat with my parents and their good friends; while, all the time, I was sporting footwear piled high with sick. It was enough to make me ill all over again.

My favourite part of the whole sorry incident is that my mother and father never mentioned what had happened. Why confront something when it can be ignored? At least, I assume that was their way of making me squirm for ever, and not a sign that they hadn't fully understood what had happened and somehow thought my shoes were some kind of fashion statement.

Happily, I rarely travel by bus these days. I can remember many a hideous journey spent on the night bus. Sometimes I would wake up at the station at the end of the route or, one night, I remember I just kept waking up on Kingsway in London but each time I did, the bus was travelling in a different direction. To make things worse, I have never lived anywhere near Kingsway.

The very first time I appeared on Radio 4's *Loose Ends* we all went to the pub afterwards. This happened every week and Ned Sherrin, the host, always bought the first round and then paid for it with a cheque. The show finished at eleven on Saturday morning so we were always sat with a pint or a glass of wine by half past at the very latest. There were a few plates of sausage rolls and bowls of crisps but nothing that my Irish friend would have recognised as 'soakage'. Daytime drinking can be very dangerous and I feel that in my excitement at doing the show, I got a little carried away. Blinking into the sunlight, I emerged from the pub at four o'clock in the afternoon and staggered off to find the number 38 bus to get me back to my flat in Hackney. If I had simply fallen asleep I wouldn't even bother you with this tale. What made it remarkable was that when I woke up I was no longer on the bus. I was in bed. It was not my bed and I was not alone. I began to understand why they called the show *Loose Ends*. After that I was a little more careful with my lunchtime consumption of the grape.

Over the years I have sometimes appeared to be outrageous and I'm sure some of the things I have done on television have shocked viewers of a sensitive nature, but in my personal life I am

185

not a rule breaker. If the sign says 'Keep off the grass' then that is what I will do. I think it is less to do with conforming and far more to do with not wanting to be told off. I am my mother's son and she did not raise me for rebellion. All of this meant I very rarely attempted to get served in pubs before I was eighteen. After that, it was almost as if I was making up for lost time.

* * *

Two years of university was enough for me. Initially it had been fabulous, but then I found myself becoming deliberately isolated and wallowing in my unhappiness. It was as if I had checked out before I had physically left. All too soon, Cork had started to feel as claustrophobic as Bandon and I had to get out.

Running away to America seemed like the most exciting plan. I would be free there. I could reinvent myself and do anything I wanted to. Unfortunately, no one told me that the drinking age in San Francisco was twenty-one. I was twenty. Of course I did have drinks, but very rarely in bars, unless I happened to be out with older friends who could get served for me.

In the March just before my twenty-first birthday I was getting a little more confident, not to mention impatient, so on St Patrick's Day I joined a bunch of people from work at a local bar full of city types. Because of the day and, I presume, due to lack of actual incidents, a local news crew was in the bar interviewing people. My friends dragged them over, pointing at me.

186

'He's Irish! Talk to him!'

Secretly delighted, I slurred some nonsense at the preppy reporter and thought no more about it. When I returned to the hippy commune where I was living, Erica, the house matriarch, greeted me with much excitement. 'You're on the news!'

'What? Why?'

'I don't know. You were in a bar!'

We sat and waited for the next bulletin. It turned out the nice TV crew hadn't been doing a piece on the feast of Saint Patrick. We sat watching in mounting horror a report on the perils of drink-driving, which ended with a large close-up of my sweaty face yelling into the camera: 'I'm going to drink and drink and then go home and get sick.' It appeared to the casual viewer that I was little better than a serial killer. An early lesson in the importance of the edit.

I remember the excitement on my birthday when I was going to be able to have my first legal drink in California. I took my passport (it was to be many years before I got a driving licence) and headed with my friend, James, to a gay bar in the Haight-Ashbury area of the city. I walked up to the counter, ordered vodka tonics and braced myself for the inevitable interrogation about my age — this time, I was ready for him. The barman looked at me and started to fill two glasses with ice. Nothing! This was so unfair — first their laws had taken away my right to drink, and now they were robbing me of the satisfaction of finally being legal!

★ ★ ★

There must be a part of me that doesn't want to conform, however. Having travelled halfway around the world to the gayest city on earth, one might have assumed I would use the opportunity to start my sexual life with men . . . but no. I started dating a girl. Her name was Elizabeth and she was far too good for me. I can't really remember why she worked in the same restaurant as I did because she came from a very wealthy background. In theory she was a student at Berkeley University across the bay, but she seemed in no rush to finish her degree. Her parents had divorced and she now lived with her grandparents in a beautiful house on a very upmarket street near the Presidio Golf Course. She readily identified herself as a WASP, a white Anglo-Saxon Protestant, and dressed in the preppy manner of that tribe: short, blonde bobbed hairstyle, a tasteful string of pearls, and usually a low heel. Ralph Lauren would have been very happy to see her in his collection. What she saw in me — an effeminate young Irishman with badly bleached hair and ill-fitting loud suits that stank of moth balls, I'll never know. Perhaps dating me was just her way of being a rebel without having to get her nose pierced. Given that she was about the same age as me it was extraordinary the amount of poise and confidence she had. We were from different worlds, and hers came with a very particular set of rules, the first being: 'Apart from a Bloody Mary, never order a drink with a name.'

I have no idea why this rule existed or what it

meant but I have adhered to it over the years. Occasionally I've had a Cosmopolitan or a Negroni, but don't bother showing me the cocktail menu. I think Elizabeth's point was that the recipe should be in the title, so ordering a spirit with a mixer was fine — you could even add a splash of something or a slice of fruit — while asking for something called a Cucumber Dilly Dally not only made you sound stupid, but the chances of it not tasting the way you expected it to were very high.

The other bit of drinking etiquette I acquired from Elizabeth, which I also still use today, is a quick and easy test to see how drunk you are. Just attempt to put your elbow on the very edge of the table. It sounds simple but try it. If you miss or your arm slips then you have had enough. The only problem with it for being a way of finding out if you are inebriated is that if it turns out you are drunk, it is already too late to do anything sensible about it. As tests go, it is about as useful as finding out you don't enjoy roller-coasters once you are on one — hang on, because this probably won't end well!

In San Francisco I lived in a hippy commune. To begin with this had been because of the very cheap rent but as the months went by, I became very fond of the dozen or so people I was living with and discovered quite a lot about myself — even though I was never able to fully embrace their very principled approach to life: most of the residents were vegetarian and the only alcohol that was consumed on the premises was the occasional bottle of beer. I wasn't sure they would approve of my wild nights out and in the mornings, I was very good at disguising my hangovers. I'm one of those annoying people who never feels that bad the next day. Certainly a hangover has never meant I phoned in sick for work or missed a session at the gym. One morning I was having my breakfast at the infinity table — a giant wooden cable spool that could be expanded to seat as many people as necessary. Various housemates came and went, grabbing coffee or a bagel as they made their way out of the house and, one by one, they all asked me if I was all right. I assured them that I was feeling fine. I finished my cereal and washed the bowl and spoon before heading to the bathroom to brush my teeth. The face that stared back at me from the mirror came as a bit of a shock. All down one side of my head was dried vomit. Suddenly it all came flooding back. The night before, I had staggered in hideously drunk and had fallen asleep fully dressed on the floor of my room, far too out of it to attempt climbing the ladder up to my platform bed. At some point I must have vomited and then decided to get undressed and climb up to bed. Obviously, in pulling my jumper over my head, I had managed to smear half my face with the aforementioned debris. Such was my youth that I don't even remember being very embarrassed. I just washed it off, ready to do it all again.

The vomiting may have stopped but the sleeping continues. I don't really need Elizabeth's elbow test because when I've had enough my body just shuts down. If I make it home it is quite a regular occurrence for me to end up on the kitchen floor or even the dog bed. My rationale for this is that my bedroom is three floors up and because Bailey the labradoodle is very large, so is his bed. Far worse are the nights I don't quite make it home before sleep takes me. Fairly recently I was at a friend's birthday drinks at a tiny tequila bar in Shoreditch. I had to work the next morning so, being sensible, I left before the others to get a cab home. About forty minutes later my friends came out of the bar to find me fast asleep, leaning against a lamppost. Not a good look.

I should also take this opportunity to apologise to all the taxi drivers who have driven me home over the years. I've never been sick on the seats but I have done a great deal of sleeping. However, one of the perks of being off the telly is that no matter how incoherent or comatose I am, the driver can radio his friends and find out where I live. Once this backfired, though, when I woke up to find myself outside a house I hadn't lived in for about five years.

I really do think my home address should be part of the Knowledge exam.

★　★　★

When I started doing stand-up around the pubs and clubs in the early nineties I still abided by the rules drilled into us at drama school: any use of drink or drugs, no matter how right it felt, was the enemy of performance. I always did my

191

shows stone-cold sober but afterwards my good friends would tell me that I seemed a little nervous, and indeed I had been. Obviously nerves can be a good thing, but no audience wants to see your fear.

One night, I was asked by a friend who worked for some branch of the Australian Tourist Board to give a comic speech to some travel agents at a drinks reception. It is the sort of job I would run a mile from now: no real stage, no proper introduction, just a microphone in the middle of a brightly lit room.

Because there was no backstage I also had to stand and mingle with the other guests beforehand, so I found myself holding a glass of wine. Waiting for the awful moment to arrive I took a few sips. Perhaps it was because of the adrenaline or nerves, but I could feel the wine entering my system and precisely what it was doing to me. I'd probably had half a glass when I was called on to address the throng. It went incredibly well. There were no nerves; I had never given such a confident, polished performance.

Of course I was aware that this must have happened to many performers before me — and suddenly, without realising it, you are stumbling onto the stage drunk and nobody wants to hire you. I vowed that night that one glass would be my cut-off point and if I ever found myself having a top-up then I would stop completely. That was over twenty years ago and I still sit on my chat show with my one and only glass of wine, which most weeks never comes close to being finished. After the recording, of course, all bets are off and show nights often end up getting quite messy but if I had to choose between booze and work — and they both get a chapter in this book — I would pick work, without hesitation.

★ ★ ★

Having trained as an actor I assumed my life would be spent in digs while I travelled the country performing in regional theatre, or climbing bleary-eyed into the back of a car to be whisked off at the crack of dawn to some location or other for filming. This didn't happen. Yes, I had a few auditions and even got a couple of jobs but it was not the life of a jobbing actor I had imagined. I remember up until very recently in interviews telling journalists that no matter what level of success I achieved in other fields, I would go to my grave a failed actor. No matter how much I'm enjoying a film, TV show or theatrical performance, there is always a little part of me that is jealous I'm not in it — and, of course, an enormous part of every other audience member that is very grateful.

When I did finally make my way back onto the boards in 2009, I found that the acting world's attitude to my drinking was very different. Maybe it was because, on TV, my name is in the title of the show and I can, to a greater or lesser extent, do what I want, but on stage, appearing in the musical *La Cage aux Folles*, I was just a member of the cast answering to a director and a company manager. It was that weird time between Christmas and New Year and we were back in rehearsal for the show. I was part of a group that would be taking over from the original cast. I knew my lines and had sung the songs with a piano but we still had about three weeks of rehearsal left. News reached us that the lead, Douglas Hodge, who was playing the part I was preparing for, was off sick, so his understudy Adrian Der Gregorian would be going on — except he was off with an illness as well. The alternate cover was already on covering for the other lead, Denis Lawson, who was also confined to his sick bed. There seemed to be no choice but to cancel the fully booked performance and send the audience, many of whom had travelled quite long distances, back home.

While we were having a lunch break I noticed the producer, Sonia Friedman, talking to the director, Terry Johnson. They seemed to be glancing in my direction quite a bit. Finally they approached me with expressions on their faces that seemed to suggest one of them had accidentally driven over one of my dogs. How to break the news? Between the two of them, they finally coughed up their question — would I be willing to go on that night? Much later, Terry told me that if I had known anything about the theatre I should have said no. But on the proviso that I got to at least sing the songs with the band beforehand, I said yes.

I'm ashamed to admit that I love situations like this. I relish it when a guest pulls out at the last minute or someone refuses to take part in an item. Everyone working together against the odds. It's exciting and most of all it's fast. Now, costumes were pinned to fit me, lines were run, bits of choreography practised, and then there I was, sitting in my small basement dressing room. After the frenzy that had gone before, suddenly everything was still and I began to get an inkling of the enormity of the challenge I was taking on. A knock on the door. Terry and the company manager, Ian Wheatstone, stuck their heads into the room. They had the air of visiting someone on death row.

'Is there anything we can get you?' Terry asked.

'Oh, a glass of white wine would be lovely, please,' I replied without thinking.

The request was nothing to do with the extraordinary circumstances; it was simply my pre-show routine. But the look that Ian and Terry exchanged made it very clear that this was not the done thing in the theatre. Breaking all their rules, they smuggled a glass backstage and on I went.

I'm sure quite a lot of things went wrong that night but my sense of elation at the curtain call was never matched. However, having done that one performance, whatever itch I'd been trying to scratch was gone and really I could have walked away from the theatre completely content. Unfortunately, I had to do it seven times a week for the next four months.

During the run I abided by the teetotal pre-show rule. To be honest, I'm not sure any amount of wine could have numbed my nerves before each show, but a few sips would have been nice. I never completely understood the total ban. I was only going to be singing and dancing; it wasn't as if I was performing brain surgery or operating heavy equipment. Obviously after the show I went out but even then I couldn't go crazy. As a non-singer playing the lead in a musical I had no choice but to take care of myself.

I enjoyed the camaraderie of being part of a company and when the show went well, it was a joy, but the main thing I took away from my return to theatre was an enormous appreciation of my life: television reaps much greater financial rewards, it isn't as time-consuming and, perhaps most importantly of all, I was better at it. For the first time in my life, I appreciated the set of skills I had developed over the years and didn't feel like a failed actor. In fact, I didn't feel like an actor at all.

My last performance in the musical was also influenced by alcohol. The night after my final curtain call I was supposed to be hosting the BAFTAs. I immediately saw a problem. How could I go out after my last show and let rip for the first time in four months if I was working the next day? The truth was I couldn't. I solved the problem by extending my run for a week. What could possibly go wrong?

The problem was that having hosted the awards show at the Royal Festival Hall on the Southbank, I got a little over-excited. For a brief period my ex, Ben, was back on the scene so he was there as well. The wine flowed freely, and no one could accuse us of not taking full advantage of it. At one stage I remember a woman coming up to say hello. It turned out that she worked for Waitrose and that is where I often do my shopping. I spoke at such length about which products I liked and what I thought of the new store layout that eventually she had to make her excuses and leave, presumably hoping that the next conversation she had wouldn't be so monumentally boring.

Far later than was wise, Ben and I fell into a taxi and headed back to my house. It was a fine night and we took a bottle out to sit by the river. I'm sure some romantic words were uttered (unless, of course, I was still going on about the Waitrose ready-meal involving lamb shank and red wine). Back in the house, as I bounded down the wooden staircase, a lethal combination of brand-new formal shoes, an uneven surface and the municipal swimming pool of wine I had consumed meant that I found myself flying through the air in slow motion.

There is always time to think during a fall. The wishing it hadn't happened but most of all the hoping that the landing isn't too bad. This was hopeless. I landed on my back, hitting the stairs with the full weight of my body. It was instant agony. Ben tried to help but I begged to be left alone. Slowly adrenaline and the great torrents of wine flowing through my veins began to take the pain away. We made it to bed and I even think we managed to do some other things as well, which in retrospect is a miracle worthy of inclusion in the New Testament.

The second I woke up I knew things weren't right. The slightest movement and I could feel my ribs rubbing against each other. I was in agony. Ben left for work and I called a cab to take me to A&E.

The x-ray confirmed my worst fears: I had broken three ribs.

As anyone who has had a similar injury will know, there really isn't anything you can do about broken ribs — it's simply a case of waiting for them to mend and not doing anything too strenuous. I phoned Ian at the theatre and explained that one of the things I wouldn't be doing that night was the show. Adrian got to go on.

This was my final week and I didn't want it to end this way. I was desperate to get back on stage and say a proper farewell to the role and the cast. I went to a specialist doctor and explained my predicament. He prescribed the most powerful painkillers in the world but gave me an ominous warning about how addictive they were, telling me to be very careful and to only stay on them for as long as necessary. Duly warned, I expected to feel some sense of euphoria but none came. I simply stopped feeling the pain from my ribs and I was able to complete my last four shows. I wondered where the buzz was. Why would anyone get addicted to these pills? The answer became horribly clear when I stopped taking them a few days later: diarrhoea, nausea, headaches. The addiction was based on trying to feel normal, not high, which struck me as an incredibly dull habit to develop.

Drugs have, of course, crossed my path from time to time but for me it has always been about the bottle. It's easy to buy, I can consume it in public and it doesn't involve hanging around street corners waiting for some Range Rover with blacked-out windows to pull up.

In short, my anti-drug stance isn't a moral one, it's simply laziness.

★　★　★

I'm aware the stories I'm telling about my relationship with booze aren't very cute and the ones in these pages are just the tip of the ice cube in my life of drink. The big question is: do I have a problem? On one level I obviously do because I drink far too much but on the other hand, my rationale would be: where's the harm? Yes, it makes me fatter than I'd like to be and perhaps I would sleep better if I occasionally went to bed sober, but my work has never suffered because of drinking and surely life would seem a little dull with no vices at all. Take booze away, and how will I get my cheap kicks then?

I have actually been to a few meetings of Alcoholics Anonymous. My friend Carrie Fisher, she of Princess Leia fame, was letting me use her guesthouse in Los Angeles. Her problems with addiction are well documented, particularly in her own brilliant books, so she is still a regular attendee of AA meetings.

I went along expecting it to be full of depressed people extolling the evils of drink and, to be honest, I was dreading it. Instead, I found a room full of people who had bonded because they had all fallen in love with the same thing and, to a certain extent, they were still in love. They told nostalgic stories about their crazy nights and how low they had been dragged by alcohol. The room filled with the laughter of recognition as they eulogised the one great love of their lives.

Part of my reluctance to accompany Carrie to the meetings was my fear that I would realise I was the same as these people. But although we did share some of the same stories, I realised we had reached a very different ending. I prefer my life with booze in it, but the members I met didn't have that choice to make. They couldn't live their lives if drink remained in it. Somehow they had given alcohol all the power, and having a drink was no longer something they did — it was all they did and thought about.

I may abuse it, but my relationship with booze is still based on enjoyment rather than fear. It goes back to the pre-show glass of wine — I know exactly why I'm drinking it and while I may end up flailing around a dance floor like a member of the living dead, I like to think that I am in control of the bigger picture.

Of course, I may be wrong.

★ ★ ★

The science-fiction wailing of my phone wakes me once more. This time there are no shadows on the ceiling as technically it is still the middle of the night. I was covering the Chris Evans Breakfast Show on Radio 2 while Chris took a fortnight's holiday. I made my way down to the kitchen through the dark, quiet house. The very bricks and floorboards seemed to be aware that no one should be stirring. I set about making some breakfast. The tea poured, I opened the fridge and returned to my steaming mug. I looked down and realised that I wasn't holding the milk — I had grabbed a bottle of white wine. That tells you all you really need to know about my relationship with booze: when in doubt, grab a drink. When in joy, or sadness, or boredom, grab a drink.

Booze can be a very tricky friend or lover. I don't enjoy waking up when I fall off the kitchen counter where for some reason I decided to make my bed, but for me that is a small price to pay for the hours of fun that preceded it — the raucous laughing, the wild stories, the crazy decisions all make up my favourite nights. Just as you can't know what happiness is without experiencing sadness, so it is being sober without being drunk. It is all very well being in control all day and trying to steer your life in the right direction and maximise your potential, but what is the point if you can't release the inner moron? If you haven't experienced altered states, how do you know what state you are in? True, I can't remember every little thing that happens during an evening, but my memory will be a montage full of smiling faces filmed through a golden lens. The reality was probably a group of sweaty grey faces spraying spittle as they shouted their garbled *bon mots* at each other but I didn't experience that, and you don't have to either. Just grab a drink. Cheers!

6

Men

Relax. I'm just as worried about this as you are. Thinking about my own sex life is as unappetising to me as it is to anyone else, so rest assured things won't get too graphic. My hand will never slide down the sweat-soaked hair of his rippled body until it reaches his throbbing manhood, nor will the waves of my salty love-spume crash against the rugged coastline of his jaw . . . This is simply a quick trawl through some of the men that have been part of my life. All of them have made me happy, a few have made me cry, and none of them have turned out to be the one.

There is an old movie called *The Yellow Rolls-Royce* and, one Sunday night, RTÉ — the Irish television station — played it. I was still at primary school so I imagine I was around ten or eleven years old. Why a boy that age would watch this film is a bit of a mystery but then there was only one TV channel at the time. The story involves the titular car and three different owners. In the middle section Shirley MacLaine plays a gangster's moll who falls in love with a street photographer played by Alain Delon. There are various beautiful sequences as they drive around the south of France in the gangster's yellow car and at one point they go to the beach. I remember that as Alain Delon slipped his shirt off to reveal an impossibly smooth and tanned back it took my breath away. I may even have gasped. It was such a powerful image to me and I remember that it made me feel very peculiar but not in any way I could have articulated at the time. The most I could have told you was that I wanted to touch it, but then another part of me would have simply said that I wanted to *be* it. It was such an innocent image but for some reason incredibly sexually powerful to me. Nowadays, so much male flesh is on display in advertisements and films but in the seventies, people were only just starting to get used to the sight of women with their pale breasts exposed to the world. Of course, I was fascinated to see all that too, but none of it packed the emotional and physical punch of Alain's golden shoulders.

It is almost impossible to imagine what it was like growing up gay in a world where homosexuality didn't exist. Until the age of eighteen or nineteen, I would never have identified myself as gay and even after that, the most I could bring myself to accept was that I might be bisexual. Obviously I knew I was different, but because I was an outsider for many reasons, it wasn't till much later and after hearing the stories of other gay men who had grown up in similar circumstances that I fully realised that I had been gay all along. People thought I was joking when I said on an Irish chat show that I just thought me feeling out of step was because I was a Protestant, but it's true. Being a Protestant in the deep, dark jungle of Roman Catholic Ireland was enough to make anyone feel alien. What I hadn't quite understood was the fact that even within our small church community I didn't fit in, and Alain Delon's shoulders didn't feature in testaments old or new.

Some gay men discover sex very young but I wasn't one of them. Of course when I was at boarding school there was a bit of fooling around but it was all very tame. At no time did I have an experience with another boy that involved any sort of real sexual act. Thirty years later, handing out the prizes at my school, I was astonished to shake hands with out gay students. I'm sure coming out in Bandon, Co. Cork, is still not very easy but at least now it is an option.

The first time anything approaching sex raised its purple head was when I was a sixteen-year-old foreign-exchange student in France. A pale young man called Claude stayed with me and my family for a month and then, when he returned home, I accompanied him for a second month. In Ireland I only remember the two of us being very bored. I wasn't what could be described as an active child, nor did I have many friends. None of this bothered me since I was very happy to spend my days reading books and watching TV but when you suddenly have a brooding shadow who doesn't even share your language, this lifestyle seemed woefully inadequate. The long afternoon that myself and my mother spent watching the wedding of Charles and Diana was particularly tense. While tears rolled down our faces watching the beautiful meringue being transported by carriage through London, a very grumpy Frenchman sat in the corner muttering oaths in his mother tongue that I was very glad my mother's ears couldn't understand.

My parents had been dreading our Gallic visitor because of all the horror stories from other families who had hosted French youths in previous years. 'They eat nothing!' 'He went missing for three days!' Of course, shiny Claude proved the exception to the rule and politely consumed every plate of grey meat or bowl of Instant Whip my mother put in front of him. And never left my side.

All too soon my parents were waving me off at the airport. The last thing that my mother said to me was, 'Eat everything.' I understood that I was no longer eating for myself; I was eating for Ireland. The reputation of a nation rested upon my being able to swallow cheese that smelt like it had been around since the Revolution.

The month in France passed pleasantly enough. The sun shone every day and, unlike me, Claude had all sorts of interests: tennis, cycling, windsurfing — for four weeks I experienced what it was like to be a healthy, active young man. It was hard to admit but I quite enjoyed it.

About three or four days before the end of my stay, Claude and I were getting changed after windsurfing on the local lake. I couldn't help but notice that my French friend seemed quite excited. Like any polite young man from West Cork I chose to ignore it and thus spare him any embarrassment. It soon became clear, however, that whatever emotions were coursing through Claude's veins, embarrassment wasn't one of them. He waved his penis around like a fleshy baguette straight from the oven. I could hear him saying things in French as he pointed to it, but my brain was in no state to be doing translation. I gathered my clothes like a flustered nun who had stumbled into a monastery by mistake and fled.

For my last weekend we went camping in the Pyrenees and, sure enough, as soon as the lights were out so was the baguette. This time there was no avoiding it. Given the number of baked goods I've handled since then, I find it astonishing how deeply shocked and ashamed I was by my own behaviour. I blamed Claude entirely, and never allowed myself to admit that I had been just as keen and excited. I returned home weighed down by my terrible secret and guilt. I even wrote poetry.

I was far from gay.

Ultimately, I never really made the decision to come out. The world did it for me. At university, even though I had girlfriends, I found that when a new friend looked serious and said, 'Can I ask you something?' it was invariably a question about my sexuality, to which I would stutter some vague, implausible reply about being attracted to people, not their gender. When the French professor I had an affair with accused me of being gay by storming off in a huff I inadvertently proved her point.

Living in the hippy commune in San Francisco I felt my sexuality was of less interest. This was a free-wheeling broad church where labels were never encouraged. One night, when I was walking home from the cinema with my favourite hippy, a dark bearded man called Obo, he asked if he could pose me a question. I assumed it would be the old chestnut about my sexuality. Instead he dived right in with, 'Would you like to spend the night with me?' I couldn't have been more surprised. Oh wait, I could . . . Just then a car slowed down and some local youths leaned out the window to yell, 'Faggots!' I really was the last to know.

Of course I did sleep with sweet Obo but the complication there was that he wasn't actually gay. He felt that everyone was 'pansexual' so acted accordingly but, deep down, I'm pretty sure he was an old-fashioned conventional heterosexual.

My last attempt at finding my own heterosexual within meant that I spent most of my year in San Francisco dating the fragrant Elizabeth, with her wealthy family and her preppy ways. After I returned to Europe we attempted to keep the relationship going — long epistles in tiny, cramped writing filled those pale blue airmail letters where the envelope and contents are all in one. Tissue-thin and difficult to read, they were like an airborne clue to how hard it would be to maintain a romance across the oceans. Phone calls were prohibitively expensive and hard to schedule and flights were not things people took lightly. We ignored all the evidence to the contrary and pledged that we could make it work. We were in love and it would be for ever.

Looking back now, I can't simply blame the innocence of youth because I still attempt to have relationships with an ocean in the way, but at least now everyone has a mobile phone and I can throw money at the problem with frequent flights.

However, of course the inevitable happened, and Elizabeth drifted into the arms of a Persian prince.

'You mean Iranian,' I spat down the phone when she broke the news.

It is never nice to be dumped but this felt more like being cut adrift. I left the shores of heterosexuality behind me, and set sail for where I should have been all along.

I had come to London to attend drama school and was paying my way by working in a large basement restaurant in Covent Garden. As all talk of Elizabeth faded I found that every new waiter or waitress just assumed I was gay and I didn't say or do anything to contradict them. After about a year I was a fully out gay man living in London, but without once having had an awkward conversation or heart to heart with anyone.

Two men dominated my life at this point. First there was Syd — beautiful, doomed Syd. Typing those three simple words thirty years later and I find I am in tears once more. Syd will always have a satin-lined corner of my heart where he will live on for ever. I say his name and his beautiful smile burns so brightly in my mind's eye that it hurts. He was a Canadian living and working in London and I fell hopelessly in love with him. Weeks went by with me trying to find ways to simply stand near him and looking for signs that he liked me where there were none. He touched my shoulder when he got off the night bus. He laughed at my jokes. He asked if I wanted the last of the leftovers. It was all in my imagination but before I could comprehend what was going on, I was in way out of my depth.

It was the darkest part of winter and more than once I remember battling the wind and rain as I crossed Waterloo Bridge, the lights of my new home city blurred by my tears. Like a wounded animal I howled into the night sky. Young hearts don't break; they explode with operatic intensity. Eventually, spurred on by a trip to a tarot-card reader, I plucked up the courage to ask Syd if he wanted to spend the night with me. I knew what his answer would be but I needed to know for sure. He broke his 'no' to me as sweetly as possible and after my initial humiliation, our relationship blossomed into a proper friendship. He became my unofficial mentor as I took my first tentative steps into the big, bad gay world that London offered. We went clothes shopping together. He introduced me to the concept of skincare. We went clubbing, we laughed and I managed to somehow control my undying love.

After a couple of years Syd headed back to Canada. He told us it was just for a holiday but then the weeks grew into months. Why wasn't he coming home? Eventually, two of his closest Canadian friends took me out to lunch and broke the news: Syd was sick. Syd would not be coming back. Sweet, sexy, beautiful, funny Syd.

AIDS had great taste. It cherry-picked a generation, leaving behind friends and families clinging to each other in their hastily assembled funeral outfits. We didn't know how to say goodbye. Why would we? Young and finding our way in eighties London — this was our beginning. How was it possible that this was the end of someone's story?

Even worse than the goodbyes were the phone calls we would get late at night in the restaurant from a frightened Syd in a hospital ward, thousands of miles away. His garbled conversation wouldn't make sense, perhaps because of his medication or maybe he had developed some sort of dementia but then, like the sun appearing from behind the darkest bank of clouds, his voice would steady and our Syd would re-emerge to tell each of us how much he loved us. Openly sobbing, we told him that we loved him too. Abruptly the line would go dead as he ran out of coins for the payphone, and we would head back to our tables to politely enquire if people would care for dessert.

Since then I've bid premature farewells to far too many friends. It always seems that somehow we should find some sort of life lesson in these pointless deaths. Invariably people spout platitudes about never taking life for granted, or living each day as if it were your last, but if I'm honest, all I take away from these bleak goodbyes is the knowledge that life is unbearably cruel and random. I'm not a believer myself but if there is a god, he is playing darts with a blindfold on, and nobody appears to be keeping score.

When my dogs, Bailey and Madge, are galloping along the beach, in love with the waves and their own speed, then I feel like I'm a winner; but listening to a friend play the piano at his wife's funeral and it feels like the game, whatever it may be, is over. No rules, no promises, no expectations. If you can't roll with the punches you shouldn't be here.

★ ★ ★

After that rather morbid detour, let me return to men and the other man who dominated those early London years. After my aborted attempts to hook up with Syd I simply assumed that I'd remain on the shelf. I felt gay shoppers would not be interested in this item. When I look back at pictures of myself, it breaks my heart that I

212

was so unconfident! I looked good back then, but then there will probably come a time when I look at pictures of myself today and wish that I still looked like this.

Of course, everyone knows that just when you are feeling truly resigned to being alone, that is when love decides to walk down the basement stairs and apply for a job as a waiter . . . Pale blue eyes looked out from under a floppy fringe as he smiled with a cute upside-down grin and introduced himself: 'I'm Ashley,' he said, with an accent that was unmistakeably Australian.

I did find him attractive but more than anything I found him funny and, rather pleasingly, he seemed to laugh a great deal whenever he was around me. In no rush to be humiliated, there was little chance that I was going to make the first move so a complicated, time-consuming courtship commenced. It must have been fairly clear I was interested — I was like an antelope feigning a limp at the waterhole, hoping the lion would pounce — but nothing was happening. Finally, late one night while I was boring him with photo albums from my time in San Francisco, he turned and asked, 'What would happen if I kissed you?' I didn't answer. The antelope just threw himself at the king of the jungle.

After that things moved very fast. I had never felt like this before; this was what truly being in love and happy felt like! Within a couple of months we were sharing a flat on Old Brompton Road. That may sound rather grand, but it was a basement apartment and we were sharing with

213

about five girls from Oz. And it had only one bedroom. I don't know if this is still a thing but at the time, it was the Australian way — they may come from a wild, under-populated island but when it comes to London and the prospect of paying rent, they are suddenly very happy to live like ants.

I have no recollection of the logistics but I do recall there was quite a bit of sex; but, even more than that, there was eating — one afternoon, for no good reason, Ashley and I sat in our sofa bed eating a bag of fifty mini sausage rolls. It may have been romantic but it wasn't exactly Antony and Cleopatra.

Most of my time was spent working and trying to get into drama school. By now I had failed one year of auditions but had received enough call-backs and words of encouragement that I felt compelled to try again.

This time around, almost at once, I was given a place at Central in north London. After the torturous hoops I had been forced to jump through the times before, the speed of my acceptance came as an anti-climax; I went to work at the restaurant that night with no feeling of euphoria. The fight was over and now the real work would have to begin.

It also meant that for the next three years I knew exactly where I would be and what I would be doing: Ashley not so much. I remember when he announced he would be going home how crushed and rejected I felt. I was too young to realise that there was no way I could compete with all his family, friends and sense of home.

For a second time I found myself attempting a long-distance relationship — the crumpled blue airmail envelopes fluttering onto the mat without a sound; the brief, snatched phone calls with words echoing through time delays across the hemispheres.

As a brand-new full-time student I was given a credit card, which I had never had before and, it turns out, should probably have been denied. The first thing I did with it was buy a ticket to Melbourne for my summer holidays. The next thing I did with it was to continue spending.

Nobody at the bank or anywhere else had explained that the credit limit was precisely that — the limit. I had decided that at the end of each month you got that amount to spend again: no mobile phones, no computerised card machines, just nice Australians handing me carbon receipts for my purchases for two whole months. The biggest department store in Melbourne, Myer, had an enormous banner hanging outside that just said: 'Want it? Charge it!' I read that and believed it. The eighties was a great time for credit-card fraud, I just didn't know I was doing it.

When I returned home I had a surprising amount of mail. Upon closer inspection, about 90 per cent of it was from my bank. It turned out that NatWest really was the bank that cared.

During my visit, it had finally been decided that Ashley would return to London and the rest of our love-filled life could continue. As soon as I got back, I set about trying to find a suitable nest for the lovebirds. I found one in an area called

Queen's Park. It was written in the stars. Deposits were paid, moving dates agreed. It all felt so grown up and committed. It is hard to remember a time when I was as excited and happy. Then, one more pale blue envelope fluttered onto the mat.

It should have simply borne the legend 'Not Coming' smeared in his own shit, but instead it contained a long, rambling story about some woman and how she had shown him that he wasn't ready to have a relationship until he had learned to love himself. Obviously this lady was a highly trained something, but it struck me that if you wanted to learn to love yourself, maybe you shouldn't behave like an enormous dick-head.

I was devastated. Clearly I was upset that the

love of my life was walking away but it was more than that. This was about the pillows I had bought, the lamp, the ironing-board cover, the life we had been going to share for ever. We might just have been two boys play-acting at being a married couple but at the time it had felt so real. The scene had been set, but now the star of the show had quit the production.

I got on the phone and pleaded and cajoled and begged. He couldn't just throw our life away without giving us another chance. Look me in the eye and tell me that you don't want me any more! Eventually my powers of persuasion worked and Ashley agreed to come back to London one more time.

That phone call was one of the biggest mistakes of my life.

Ashley's arrival marked the beginning of six months of emotional torture. I had pleaded for my lover to return but what I got was a New-Age bore full of the teachings of an organisation called LRT, which stood for Loving Relationship Training.

They seemed to be training Ashley for a version of loving relationships that I didn't recognise: he gave me crabs. Thank you. When I was lying ill in hospital following a late-night mugging, rather than coming to visit me, he asked an LRT seminar to send me healing vibes. Too kind. He borrowed money from my friends so that he was able to attend a conference on immortality in Hawaii. Really?

All of this should have meant that I was thrilled to get him out of my life, but like a

217

lovelorn dog with a bone, I couldn't let go. I scrabbled around, desperate to unearth the funny, sweet, romantic Ashley that I had fallen in love with but eventually I had to accept that he was gone and I stopped looking. We moved out of the flat: me to a rented room in Brixton, and he back to Australia.

The chapter was closed and yet the bruising to my battered heart lived on — it would be seven years until I was finally ready to trust someone enough to use the word 'boyfriend' again. Perhaps even now, some of my difficulties in relationships stem from that early disillusionment. We were both so young that it's hard to know how much of the relationship was real and what proportion of it was in our romantic imagination, but the pain was undeniable.

About twelve years ago, Ashley was visiting London and got in touch. Fourteen years had passed since the end of our affair but walking into the restaurant in Knightsbridge for our lunch, it felt strangely like a first date.

By this stage, my show was on Channel 4 so the waiters knew me, and passers-by spotted me and banged on the window. I'm not proud of how it made me feel, but it was suspiciously close to revenge.

Meeting with any ex is never easy, and there is inevitably an invisible dance to a silent tune, but I felt I was winning. Ashley was my first love and as such will always be special, but no spark was reignited that day. As I looked across the table at this still familiar face, I was reminded of how you can touch a scar on your knee and remember the fall from your bike as a child — a glance, a laugh and I was back in that flat in Queen's Park. The heart is a tough old organ and will always recover in the end, but it never truly forgets.

★ ★ ★

The next seven years were hardly celibate; indeed, they might be best described as slutty. I had met Ashley relatively early in my gay life and now it was time to sow all those wild oats I hadn't had a chance to before. One-night stands were the order of the day, but in a world before apps like Grindr or Tinder, these trysts took time. It seemed like every night after work in the restaurant (my acting career was still not troubling my life very much) we went out to some gay club or other. It seemed so important at the time and yet I remember so few of my conquests. There was the guy who burst into tears when he came, the one that wet the bed and then locked my underwear in his faulty washing machine; then there were the fat twins, the ugly guy with a car, the dark, the blond, the old, the young, the sweet and the frightening. It can only be described as seedy and yet to all of us involved, it seemed like good, clean fun.

The first little glimmer that I was ready to date again happened when I met Eric. Tall, dark and Canadian, I always picture him in a leather jacket, wearing denim shorts to the knee and holding a skateboard. We were never going to be a perfect match but we did manage to have a little affair that lasted for about six months. It ended when I got my first paid acting gig at the Liverpool Playhouse. It was to set a pattern in my life — work comes first.

My time by the Mersey was what I thought my life was supposed to be like. I was playing a small part in Sean O'Casey's *The Shadow of a Gunman*, which meant I was technically an actor but in reality had no responsibilities, so my habit of heading out every night could continue unfettered. One boy I met was very handsome, but once in the bedroom proved a major disappointment. To be perfectly blunt, his foreskin was too tight so he came almost at once. While I never enjoy people who take ages, this was hardly worth taking your pants off for. In a time before mobiles, emails or texts, I wrote a letter to a good friend back in London and included the story of my hair-triggered lover from Liverpool. A few weeks later, my friend found himself in bed with a handsome man with a thick Scouse accent and all too soon he realised it was the same man I had mentioned in the letter. It's a very small gay world.

As if to prove the point, I was leaving a restaurant a couple of years ago when a man grabbed my arm: 'I'm in your book!'

I stared at him blankly.

'The man with the foreskin!' he exclaimed brightly. Of course I now remembered everything, including that my friend had had sex with him again at a later date when, following a circumcision, his performance had been much improved. I told him what my friend had told me and apologised if being in my autobiography had

220

caused him any embarrassment. At this point I hadn't paid any attention to his dining companion, but now, with a big smile on his face, he said, 'Graham, I'd like you to meet my mother.' I must have blushed, but attempted to shake her hand with the air of a man who had not just been discussing her son's new and improved penis.

I was the youngest member of the cast in Liverpool but the others soon took me under their wing. It was fairly clear I wasn't God's gift to the acting profession but I didn't waste anyone's time in rehearsals and, once on stage, managed to avoid the furniture and deliver my few lines on time.

Backstage, an actor called Desmond Jordan soon came to be my best friend. At the time he was only sixty-three but he liked to act much older. He was still very handsome, with a beautiful mane of grey hair and the facial silhouette of a classical statue but anyone could see that in his youth he must have looked like a matinee idol. Born in Dublin, Desmond had chosen to make his life in the UK.

Our friendship was very much based on the fact that we could make each other laugh like filthy drains and, before I could stop it, I realised that my heart had become engaged. Clearly nothing could happen but equally I stuck to his side like a lovesick puppy picking up the crumbs of his attention. Soon I discovered he had a boyfriend, and this was not the sort of relationship anyone could meddle with. He was an actor called Dennis Edwards, ten years

Desmond's senior, and they had been together for almost forty years. When I saw them sitting side by side sharing their stories, jokes and private glances I was so jealous — not of Dennis, but of both of them and the history they owned together. I adored Desmond and soon grew to love his boyfriend and their extraordinary bond. This was a relationship I could aspire to: not just a same-sex version of my parents; these were two handsome, funny, creative men who had found each other and had managed to never let go.

Over the years I became a sort of little project for them and they would give me advice and worry about me. They were my adopted gay parents. Like me, they both enjoyed a drink and we spent many booze-soaked nights together whenever I visited their picture-perfect antique-filled house in the seaside town of Deal. I loved hearing their stories, which transported me back to a lost theatrical world. Dennis had appeared in the film version of *The Prince and the Showgirl* with Laurence Olivier and Marilyn Monroe. Vivien Leigh, just before she became too ill, had announced she wanted him to be her new leading man. Desmond had worked consistently over the years and even starred in West End musicals. I got the impression that I wasn't the first cast mate to fall under his spell.

We come now to the 'life is cruel' portion of their tale. Of course I could see they were getting older but they still walked their dog, drank their whiskey and remained interested in everything that was going on in the wider world. Then disaster struck. Dennis had a debilitating stroke and Desmond, although he appeared very healthy, developed a severe heart condition. They made the agonising decision to sell all their antiques and the vast majority of their precious mementoes in order to move into two rooms in an old people's nursing home in the leafy wilds of north-east London.

The facility was run specifically for retired theatrical types and was as comfortable and pleasant as it is possible for such places to be — after the initial shock, I think they both came to sort of enjoy it. They liked the gossip and how professional slights from decades before could still be played out. I witnessed this first hand when I was having lunch with them in the dining room one Sunday, and a retired casting director decided to come and say hello. The detour required by the grey-haired lady to do this with her Zimmer frame seemed to take several minutes. Finally she was at the table.

She smiled at us all. 'Good afternoon.'

We returned her salutation but in the silence that followed it became clear no conversation was going to be encouraged by my old friends. Their ancient nemesis duly turned her frame, laboriously, and had barely taken one step away from us when Desmond uttered a very audible, 'Cunt.' He could still make me laugh like a drain.

Dennis hated all the indignities that had come with his stroke: the bed baths, the assistance with going to the toilet, the searching his damaged brain for the right word. When he sat in bed, looked you in the eye and said, 'I wish I'd never woken up on that bathroom floor. I should have died,' it was impossible to think of any words of comfort. When he finally went, aged ninety-two, it seemed like a blessing.

The problem was that Desmond, who by this point had been his partner for nearly sixty years, was left behind. Visiting him now was a heartbreaking ordeal. He wept almost constantly. 'How can I have so many tears in me?' he would ask in between sobs. He held my hand tightly and urged me: 'Stay single. No one should have to go through this.' I joined him in his weeping. His will to live gone, his whiskey consumption up, it wasn't long till he joined the man he had lived for.

There was no funeral. Six old friends stood on top of the white cliffs of Dover that he had loved and, after taking shots of Irish whiskey, dispatched his ashes into a cloudless blue sky. No lessons to be learned, no comfort to be had, but his unbearable pain was over.

★　★　★

Back in my own life, hopes of becoming an actor abandoned, I had drifted into doing stand-up comedy. I was making a meagre income and was living in a tiny one-bedroomed flat that was just off Columbia Road's flower market, in London's East End.

By now the thrill of sexual conquests seemed to have faded, or maybe I was just a bit older and fatter. Whatever the reason, more often than not I found myself climbing into an empty bed longing to find a warm body waiting with an embrace. Twenty years later, climbing into a chill, crisp bed by myself is one of the highlights of my day but this was a time before I had ever lived with a lover, or found the deep comfort of a canine snore.

One night, some friends invited me to dinner and amongst the other guests was an American man called Scott. He was tall and well built with close-cropped hair and a small beard. I found myself drawn to him. It is never clear what creates an attraction. Did I like this man simply because I didn't fancy anyone else at the dinner? Was I allowing myself to like him because he lived out of reach in Los Angeles? No one can explain why Cupid's arrow hit such a bull's eye that night, but it did. I have also tried to convey to friends Scott's killer chat-up line but nobody else, even though all my friends adored him, has ever really understood why it grabbed me so completely.

After dinner, we all went to a gay bar in nearby Islington and Scott, standing very close to me at the bar, asked: 'Are you drunk?'

'No.'

'Would you like to be?'

With that line and a smile, I was his for the next five years.

Long distance. It can't be a coincidence that somebody writing about their love affairs should write that phrase so often. I can blithely explain it away by saying I like accents, but it is probably more to do with a fear of complete commitment — I allow myself to open my heart, safe in the knowledge that they will leave me. At least this time there were no blue envelopes, as we were in the exciting age of the fax machine! White waves of paper would crash down onto the cheap carpet shore of my living room with sentimental love notes and press clippings he thought I might enjoy. And this time, there was less time delay on the phone line and the bills weren't quite as frightening.

Money was to be in my very near future but when I met Scott that really didn't seem likely as sporadic stand-up gigs and bits of radio were my only income. Scott was running a tour-guide business and was by no means wealthy but he had more than I did. When I went to visit him for Christmas it was only because I was able to borrow some money from friends.

The trip was an emotional leap of faith but I came home sure of two things: I really loved Scott — gentle, generous, funny, sexy Scott; and I had no idea how I was going to pay my friends back.

Within a couple of weeks, however, my financial future seemed much brighter. First, I got a part in the sitcom *Father Ted* and, while I was rehearsing that, I found out that I was going to be the sidekick to Maria McErlane for twenty-six episodes of Cher's favourite late-night sex-quiz, *Carnal Knowledge*. Suddenly, I had more money than I had dreamt of! For my thirty-third birthday I had a party in a room above a pub and I was able to put enough cash behind the bar to pay for drinks all night. If I never earned another penny I didn't care. This was my thank you to all my friends who had stuck with me through my days of penury and failure. It felt great.

As if I had used up all our luck, Scott suddenly found himself in Los Angeles without a job. I was now hosting a show for the fledgling Channel 5 and my bank balance was continuing to grow, so the solution to Scott's problem seemed obvious: he should move to London to be with me.

Of course there were some things to be sorted out first. Scott was one of those old-school Americans who was very concerned by the size of our fridges and the state of our plumbing, so I moved into a smart new apartment that had both a fridge-freezer and a power shower. The UK couldn't have made my boyfriend more welcome. But the problem with me being able to pay for all of this was that it meant I was very busy working. Scott moved to London to be with me, only to find that I was out all the time. In addition, there was the complication of people beginning to recognise me. Nothing I was doing could be considered mainstream but still, it became the norm for us to be joined by random strangers whenever we went out for a drink. This was all new to me so I was unsure how to handle it. I felt I couldn't be rude or blunt with these people, so it was left to Scott to be the bad cop. As time went by and my fame grew, things became worse, with people blatantly ignoring Scott or even pushing past him to get to me. Add to this toxic situation the fact that Scott was unable to work and you have one very unhappy, resentful boyfriend.

Having longed for the sort of success and recognition I was now getting, I found I couldn't really enjoy it. My joy was Scott's pain. As the relationship began to crumble, certain friends criticised Scott's inability to cope with my career or even his jealousy of it, and I was happy to join in. Since then I have come to understand that it wasn't Scott's fault but a basic flaw in gay relationships when one of the partners is much more successful than the other. I meet sweet guys who are initially drawn to my wealth and lifestyle — the linen napkins and oysters, a celebrity-filled party, a flat bed in the sky. But slowly their enjoyment starts to sour. Every man, no matter how young and fey, has some alpha in them. Where the pretty young woman who marries a fat, ugly billionaire can find her role in having babies and playing hostess, my boyfriends find themselves emasculated and unhappy.

★ ★ ★

My success explains why the rest of the men in this chapter are suddenly much prettier and younger, but it is also the reason why the affairs are shorter and more incendiary.

The break-up with Scott was slow, painful and inevitable: couples' counselling, getting Scott a work permit — nothing helped. We loved each other but one's very existence made the other one unhappy. Finally the day came when he moved out.

With a sigh of relief I shut the door and began

my new life as a wealthy bachelor with his own TV show.

I thought it would be very straightforward. I was an idiot.

About four days into singledom, I found myself making out with a very attractive gentleman in a bar in south London. We exchanged numbers and decided to go on a date.

He showed up at the appointed time with a large sack and a smile. 'I've got you a surprise!'

I eyed the sack nervously. 'What is it?' I asked.

'I'll tell you when I get back from the bar.' He walked away, leaving the large bag.

I stared at it and for some reason my mind immediately went to a scenario where this guy was unhinged and my lovely gift was a kitten. I looked at the sack for any sign of movement. Was it possible he had got me a *dead* kitten?

In the event, it turned out it was a picnic. Sweet. I saw the guy a couple of times and then he fell off the edge of the planet. This can be a problem when people think they know you off the telly, as dull, unscripted reality is often a huge disappointment. The no-make-up thing probably doesn't help either.

Robert Pattinson, the heart-throb from the *Twilight* movies, tells a cautionary tale. There was a young woman who was obsessed by him — every airport he landed at she seemed to be there first; whenever he left a hotel, she was waiting by the entrance. She was never threatening or demanding, just a constant presence in his life. Once he was filming in Europe and he was all alone and very bored. As he left the hotel one night to go and find a table for one, he noticed the girl. On a foolhardy whim, he asked her if she would like to join him for dinner. Of course she agreed — her dreams had come true! They spent the evening together and, back at the hotel, he bid her a chaste goodnight. He never saw the young woman again. Be careful what you wish for — whoever she thought Robert Pattinson was obviously hadn't matched with her dinner date that night. Most fantasies should never become a reality.

* * *

I met a lot of people and although I saw several of them more than once, there was no one who really filled the role of boyfriend. Many of them have become good friends and we simply choose to ignore the carnal side of how we met. There were far too many big nights out and bleary mornings-after, but I don't regret a moment of it. I had spent nearly forty years getting to the point where I had cash in my pocket and a certain notoriety, so it seemed churlish not to enjoy it. A story a friend of mine once told me sums it up well: he was sitting with the director, Michael Winner, while Michael flicked through an album of photographs showing him with various lady friends. 'Look! The older and more hideous I get, the younger and prettier they are!' I know exactly how he feels, and I'm not proud, but the flesh is weak.

When I started working in New York, I didn't have the same amount of recognition I did at home, but occasionally on a night out people might know me from BBC America, or if the boys were very savvy, they might notice the expensive shoes and fat wallet. This isn't meant to sound self-pitying or overly cynical as I am aware of how these things work. It may seem shallow on both our parts, but for all the talk of, 'I don't care what he does. I just want someone with a great sense of humour,' it's odd how few dates the funny guy selling the *Big Issue* goes on.

★　★　★

There is a bar in New York called Barracuda. A small, unassuming door leads into a narrow bar area and then at the back it opens up into a much larger lounge room that also has a stage. Most nights of the week they have drag shows of variable quality. My favourite night was Monday, when the evening was hosted by Candis Cayne. To look at, she was all blonde bombshell; to listen to, she was a razor-tongued trucker. She lip-synched to songs and told us stories about her life. A room full of people who clearly had nothing else to do early on a Tuesday morning cheered her to the rafters.

A tall, thin man approached me at the show one week. 'You look like Graham Norton.'

'Do I?'

He laughed and I found I was smiling back at him.

'Are you Graham Norton?'

'Yes.'

He introduced himself as Kristian and we started chatting. He was there with a man he worked with at a popular chain restaurant in Times Square. The three of us headed off to Splash for a last drink. Until recently, this was the largest, busiest gay bar in the city, getting its name from the showers behind the bar where the go-go boys danced. Serving the drinks, the bartenders just wore their underpants and all of them were so well built and handsome that if any of them had ever come to Britain they would surely have been famous. I loved the place.

Our evening began to get a bit messy and before long it was suggested that the three of us would go back to my house, where we all knew what was going to happen. Sure enough it did but, as often transpires in these situations, one person got very ignored: Kristian's friend was that man. I'm not just keeping his name secret in order to protect his identity, it's also because I can't actually remember it. The one memorable thing about him, however, especially for a man in

America, was that he had more foreskin than I had ever seen. It was a bit like a shower cap made of flesh and was more than a little off-putting. Realising that things were not going to work out the way he wanted, he decided to get dressed and go. As he left he said, 'You have a beautiful home,' as if he had just been to a sophisticated cocktail party or visiting a new neighbour. I always love a compliment but given what had just been going on, I felt it was a little surplus to requirements. After all, I doubt any member of the French aristocracy ever paused to compliment the wickerwork of the basket as they made their way to the guillotine.

The drunken nights are nearly always the same; it's the mornings-after that are wildly different. Often there is some stilted conversation while both parties realise that what their drunk selves found attractive is borderline repellent in the sober light of morn. The worst-case scenario is when this grim truth is only felt by one of the hung-over revellers — invitations to brunch are rejected and plans for a busy day are quickly invented. A cameraman once told me of a scenario he had which I pray I never experience. He had brought a young lady home but in the morning not only was she not the raving beauty he remembered, she was also quite annoying, just sitting in his bed and prattling on. All his hints to get her out of his house fell on deaf ears. Finally, when her bladder led her from the room for a moment, he quickly texted a friend asking him to call him so he could use it as an excuse to get rid of this woman who wouldn't leave. He hit Send. As he tells the story, he says the oddest thing was that when he heard her phone on the bedside table let out a little yelp of delight at the arrival of a new text, he still didn't realise what he'd done. Once his overnight guest came back in the room and checked her phone, however, he was very aware of his mistake — he had not sent his complaint to a friend but, through a combination of hung-over befuddlement and subconscious passive-aggression to the woman herself. Not surprisingly she was furious, but oddly she still didn't leave — she wanted him to tell her exactly what she had done wrong and then discuss it. Be afraid, be very afraid.

My morning with Kristian was one of the good ones: relaxed and lazy and with an easy rapport. Tall and broad-shouldered with an easy smile that took up half his face, he was more attractive than I had remembered and could make me laugh. Despite this, I suspected that I was not his type and I'd probably never see him again. We went through the mandatory exchange of numbers and I released him back into the wild.

That night I was pottering around the house when I got a text. It was Kristian. Did I want some company? It turned out I did.

Many of my friends never understood my attraction to Kristian, and if he were to be judged solely on his behaviour, then I concede he was not great boyfriend material. What they couldn't see was the special spark that fires within him: when he decides to shine his light on

234

you, it makes you feel as special as he is.

Life has been a strange journey so far for Kristian. At high school he was the popular kid, picked for the teams, great at athletics, but he also had a beautiful singing voice and a real aptitude for all sorts of dancing. He entered competitions and he won them. Musical theatre was his first love but soon he began to dream of becoming a pop star. Then, because he was Kristian, he got offered the chance to join a new boy band. He jumped at the opportunity. The five boys were flown to Sweden where they recorded an album, and, back in America, they began a series of shows promoting their first single on hundreds of radio stations. Then disaster struck. The mother of the youngest member fell out with the manager and, with no warning, their dreams turned to dust and they were left to fend for themselves in Miami.

When we met he had been back in New York for about a year and paying his bills working in restaurants and bars. I think he was still in shock about what had happened and, having put all his eggs in one basket, wasn't sure what to do next. He went to dance classes, he wrote lyrics, he went to the occasional open audition for something, but nothing really stuck. He was lost when I found him and I was totally unprepared for how difficult that would make our lives.

Within three weeks of our meeting I had asked him to come with me to Cape Town. He said yes. We visited London together and he was my red-carpet date at the National Television Awards. It was what the tabloid papers would have described as a whirlwind romance. Sadly, though, whirlwinds are usually followed by storms and, sure enough, back in New York, he started to test my feelings for him.

Calls went unanswered, nights ended in drunken rows and six months after we'd said hello in that bar, I found myself saying goodbye in a Starbucks just off Times Square. Stupidly, I thought I was walking away from someone who didn't care — the look on his face told me how wrong I was, but it was too late to back down and I was angry and hurt and in return I wanted him to feel awful too. The pre-production for our new Comedy Central show was in full swing then; in fact, I can remember having to make my excuses to leave a meeting in order to go and break up with Kristian and then jump in a cab to head back to the office.

This was the 'work hard, play hard' portion of my life and I soon found things to distract me from my heartache. One of those things was a young man called Tyler Peabody Hunt III.

I was out with my friend Eddie, who was also working on my show. We were at whichever gay party we were supposed to be at on that night of the week and both of us immediately noticed Tyler. He was tall and slim, with long brown hair framing an impossibly handsome face. We stared at him like dogs in the back of a car at a McDonald's drive-thru. Later on, I was on the dance floor and there he was again. Was he looking in my direction? Was that smile meant for me? We started talking. He was a model, of course, and spoke with a very sexy southern drawl. Our faces became strangely close. I wondered if he was a little deaf. Then we were kissing. I was making out with a beautiful male model while the music played and the lights turned the whole world Technicolor. I felt as if I had been (very badly) cast in a soft porn film. We left together and ended our night sitting on my roof terrace looking at the backdrop of lights in this city where it seemed the impossible could happen.

The next morning I walked into the office with a very large grin on my face.

Eddie was waiting. 'Graham, you will never do better than that!'

I assumed that Tyler would have sobered up and laughed with his friends about the hideous old queen from Europe he had ended up with the night before, but then he called.

Of course I'd like to see him.

We arranged to meet at his place and then go on for dinner. When I reached his building on the Upper East Side I was very impressed: exposed brickwork and an under-lit staircase filled the lobby. Models were clearly getting paid very well. Up on the sixth floor, however, things weren't quite so opulent. It seemed about a dozen models shared the miniscule four-room apartment but by New York standards, that wasn't particularly bad. What made it remarkable was that each room had a strangely low ceiling, because suspended above them was an enclosed platform sleeping area reached by ladders. When a model was sleepy they had to climb up to a slot-like opening and post themselves into bed like a beautiful letter.

Those coffin-like sleeping chambers were not very conducive to sexual relations. If you didn't have a headache beforehand you certainly did afterwards, due to the amount of ceiling head-banging that went on.

As I got to know Tyler a bit better I discovered that he was another lost soul. He had been the most beautiful popular boy in his high school and no one had been surprised when he had been approached by some modelling scouts. They told him to hit the gym for a few months and then head to New York where they would make him a star. He did as he was told and duly showed up at their office — where the head of the agency decided she was going for a different look. For the first time in his young life, he had been rejected. Such is the lot of the model — the most beautiful people on the planet put themselves in a world where they are constantly told they aren't good enough.

Tyler did find an agent but, casting after casting, he sat with dozens of men just as gorgeous as he was only to be told they needed longer hair, bigger arms or bluer eyes. He managed to get one campaign for Ralph Lauren but now he was working in Abercrombie & Fitch as a greeter. Growing up in small-town America he had been promised the world, but so far adulthood had been a huge disappointment.

After my initial infatuation wore off I became aware that Tyler was a little dull and also quite erratic. He had strange mood swings and sometimes over-reacted to situations in an unsettling way. We saw less of each other but I tried to stay in touch. He decided to forget about being a model and enrolled in NYU to study interior design. I found out months later from a mutual friend that his mother had been forced to come to New York to take him home when she had begun to get strange calls from Tyler where he would tell her that he couldn't find his lungs, or about his all-night search for a paint the colour of tequila. He had needed help. I've heard since that he is now back on track and happily making his way as a designer, just not in New York. Let Tyler serve as a warning — it's a city that can break you.

By the time my show was finished and I was ready to go home I found myself back with Kristian. You would think the more times you break up with someone the less seriously you will take the relationship but the opposite is true: with each ending and beginning the knot seems to become tighter, the bond more intense. I returned to London and once more I found myself using the phrase 'long distance'. This time it was easier because I was in a position to pay for airfares and hotels. Sometimes we met in New York or London but we also tried Miami and Los Angeles, thinking that we might fare better on neutral ground.

All major life decisions should be given a great deal of thought and yet I have no recollection of why we considered it might be a good idea for Kristian to come to London to live with me. Whatever reasons we came up with, they weren't good enough. The experiment lasted for about six months and it was a disaster. I realise that even to a perfect stranger this outcome would have been glaringly obvious, but when you are in the middle of something and you are desperate for it to work, you'll try anything. The only good thing to come out of cohabitation was the arrival of the labradoodle puppy called Bailey who, it turns out, has been my longest relationship to date.

Unbelievably, even after the misery we put each other through in London, we found ourselves saying that we were dating again. I'm not sure how seriously Kristian took it this time though. Once, when I went to stay with him, his roommate innocently asked, 'How do you guys know each other?' Clearly his London-based lover was not a popular topic of conversation.

In the end it was Kristian who showed enough maturity to end it once and for all. Because the break-ups had always been my call, this seemed like a true full stop. The madness was over, but this time with no shouting or histrionics, just some slow, heavy tears shed over lunch in an empty restaurant. I walked home, finding some comfort in the fact that a man in his mid-forties could still feel such heartache.

Kristian has stumbled into a new career and is now a very successful drag queen in New York. His stage name is Tina Burner and if you get the chance to seek him out, you should. He is very good. I think the make-up and the tucking get him down, but he gets paid to show off and drink, which seems like a perfect job for him.

The last time I was in Manhattan I saw him

perform and then arranged to meet for lunch the next day. When I arrived at the restaurant Kristian was waiting for me. 'Have you eaten here before?' he asked.

'Are you joking?' I replied.

'No. Why?'

'Kristian, this is the restaurant where you dumped me!'

'Oh.' An awkward pause, followed by us both laughing for a very long time.

He was a terrible boyfriend and now he's a terrible ex-boyfriend.

* * *

Since Kristian, there have been various attempts at relationships but nothing has lasted very long. Ben and his little dog seemed like it might work but somehow neither of us was able to commit. There was a lovely South African man but we parted ways; a pretty guy with heavy eyebrows; the sex addict who wouldn't have sex; the Norwegian; the brother; the Irish one . . . they have all drifted in and out of my life. I never blame myself but it is glaringly obvious that I am the common denominator in all these failed relationships. I have to ask myself if I really want the 'happy ever after' and the answer seems to be no. I like having someone around who will come out for dinner, go for holidays and even have the occasional fumble in the bedroom, but I'm not sure I'm built for sharing my entire life and heart. Being with someone should double your joy and yet I find it halved. Nor is being alone something I fear; in fact, when offered the choice, I seem to embrace it. I hope I'm wrong and that someday a man will stride across a room and lead me into an unimagined future but as I type this, I must admit I feel fairly content being solo. I'm not pretending being alone makes me ecstatically happy but I'm not sad, and that already seems like quite a lot in life.

★ ★ ★

So, I promised you a chapter about men without graphic sex and so far I feel I haven't misled you! Forgive me, then, if I finish with a story my ex Ben told me about a bedroom mishap that happened to him.

He had just moved into the first flat he had ever bought and was understandably proud. He spent the afternoon assembling his new bed from Ikea and that night went out to celebrate. And what better way to mark this occasion than by christening his pristine bedroom? He met a man and invited him back. They were getting on very well and the previously tidy room now had clothes discarded all over the floor. They had reached a point in the proceedings where a little help was needed, so Ben reached into his beside cabinet for the lube. They continued. Almost immediately, Ben sensed something was wrong. Things were quite uncomfortable, even painful. He tried to keep going but had to admit defeat. He turned on the light and discovered that he hadn't taken lube from the drawer; he had in his hand a tube of wood glue.

Every gay relationship requires wood and glue — just not at the same time.

So here we are. This chapter on men has come to a close but I've a feeling that, in my life, the subject isn't done with just yet. I always imagined there would come a moment when one lost all interest in sex but it hasn't happened yet. I have a vision of being very old indeed, sitting up in bed surrounded by tarnished awards and yellowing press clippings, small dogs licking the spilt soup off my dressing gown. That is when I'll fall madly in love with a beautiful Brazilian nurse because of his flair when performing a bed bath. Maybe we'll marry and the very next day I can die happy, knowing that for those brief few hours I had a life partner.

It's not where the story starts; it's where it ends.

7

Work

I have three jobs that I love. I hope that since you are reading this book you are familiar with at least one of them.

Every fortnight I write an advice column for the troubled readers of the *Daily Telegraph*; Saturday mornings find me talking nonsense and playing music for three hours on BBC Radio 2; and my television chat show is part of the Friday night line-up on BBC One. Of course I have other jobs, like hosting the BAFTA television awards or commentating on the Eurovision Song Contest, but while I enjoy them too, they don't preoccupy my life in quite the same way.

I remember that at the end of my autobiography, *So Me*, which was published in 2004, I had left Channel 4 but had yet to make a single show for the BBC, and I was about to embark on a new series in America for the cable channel Comedy Central. The future was wildly uncertain and yet I never had sleepless nights about it. Part of this was clearly down to stupidity and drink, but it also stemmed from the fact that I had already overshot all my dreams and ambitions by miles. I had only ever wanted to make a living acting, or, later on, as a stand-up.

The wealth and opportunities that had come with *So Graham Norton* and then *V Graham Norton* were bewildering to me. I think I was setting off on my trek into the unknown perfectly resigned to finding failure because I had already been given far more than my fair share of success.

After we taped the first episode of *The Graham Norton Effect* for Comedy Central we were shell-shocked. The wildly enthusiastic reaction of the guests and the studio audience was so overwhelming we couldn't help but count our unhatched chickens. I imagine for the vast majority of Americans who chanced upon the show while flicking through their many channels, however, it came across as one of those sitcoms where the live studio audience is laughing hysterically while you sit on your sofa stony-faced. Oh well, not to worry — I could just go back to Britain and continue with my career there. Oh, wait. I didn't appear to have a UK show any more. Finally I did become a little anxious.

The BBC had been trying to recruit me for quite some time. I remember in the autumn of 2000 standing in a dark street outside a restaurant in Tokyo while filming a documentary for Channel 4, listening to a breathless agent on the phone telling me that the BBC had offered me £5 million. I turned it down. I know that sounds crazy but I was very happy working where I was and the only thing the corporation seemed to be offering me was money. There were no actual shows for me to do.

Four years later, things were very different. I was ready to leave Channel 4 and explore the shiny-floored world of BBC entertainment. The other thing that had changed was the amount of money on offer. I'm not sure where they had found the sack of five million pound coins, but somewhere in the intervening four years they had apparently lost it. The one thing that remained the same, though, was that they still didn't really have anything for me to do.

Even before I left New York, the BBC began to pitch me entertainment formats. When it comes to doing a new show I always ask myself, 'Would I watch it?' If the answer is no, then it is a very easy decision for me to walk away from the format. Too many people in television make shows for other people. They talk about the audience as if they were aliens, but in my mind popular television should appeal to everyone. If you can't sit down and enjoy an episode of *The X Factor* or *Doctor Who* then I'm not really sure why you would want to be working in mainstream TV. I know that if I still worked in restaurants as a waiter (surely by now I'd have reached a managerial level), I would still be watching hours of television. Growing up, the TV was more than entertainment, it was a good friend and a window to a world outside rural West Cork. For me, sitting inside the box rather than being on a couch opposite it is still a dream come true.

The first show the BBC came up with that

passed my 'Would I watch it?' test was a *Strictly Come Dancing* spin-off show called *Strictly Dance Fever*. It was essentially a dancing competition for amateurs from all over the country who would have to choreograph and perform a variety of dances in front of a panel of expert judges. I was going to be the host. I liked it because we would be piggy-backing an already very successful show; I thought the job of host was something I could do well; and, naturally, there was the possibility of having sex with some dancers. In the event, only two of those things were true and that's only if you thought I was any good at hosting it.

To link it with *Strictly Come Dancing*, Arlene Phillips was one of the judges, and alongside her was the well-known choreographer and producer Stacey Haynes; Jason Gardiner, who went on to become the panto villain on *Dancing on Ice*; and Luca Tommassini, an Italian dancer and choreographer whose greatest claim to fame was dancing the tango with Madonna in the movie of *Evita*. The five of us, accompanied by an enormous production team, travelled the country for two months auditioning hundreds of dancers.

While we discovered some very talented performers, we also unearthed a whole heap of crazy. I was astonished at the variety of people who were willing to don a leotard and roll around on the floor. There appears to be a very thin line between contemporary dance and care in the community.

My debut appearance on the BBC was also going to be my first live show, and while I pretended to be nonchalant, it was made very clear to me that if I screwed up, my future with the corporation would not be a very long one.

Saturday, 26 March 2005 dawned and off I went to Television Centre to rehearse the show. It was an exciting day to be part of the BBC because right after our programme was the much-heralded return of *Doctor Who*.

The atmosphere was different to anything I had ever experienced at Channel 4: executives roamed the corridors and there was a real sense of tradition and being part of the national broadcaster.

The live show seemed to pass off without incident. I remembered the judges' names, managed not to swear and got the programme off air on time. Backs were slapped and we prepared to film some trailers for the following week's programme.

Unbeknownst to us, on the nation's televisions, Billie Piper as Rose, the Doctor's assistant, was creeping into a dark basement. The music built the tension as she peered around corners . . . suddenly, a voice that sounded very like mine was heard saying, 'Where do you want me? Over here?'

Viewers scratched their heads and wondered why the host of *Strictly Dance Fever* was hiding in this basement. Unbelievably, some sound engineer had faded up my microphone, unaware that it was somehow still patched through to the broadcast feed. Most of the ensuing fuss involved me ruining people's enjoyment of *Doctor Who*, but what concerned me was how close I had come to ending my BBC career before it had really begun. I could have been saying anything and, given my potty mouth, the chances of me dropping an F bomb or something even worse had been very high indeed.

The following week, 2 April, we rehearsed once more and I was confident that the sound department couldn't make the same mistake twice. What could possibly go wrong? About fifteen minutes before we went live to the nation I noticed some people in suits pretending not to run. Something was up — something big.

The Pope had died. Being Irish, I assumed that the good people of Britain couldn't care less that the pontiff in Rome had gone to meet his maker, but I was very much mistaken. The BBC bosses went into full panic mode. It was no surprise when I heard that our resident Italian, Luca Tommassini, upon learning the news, had thrown himself against his dressing-room wall clutching imaginary rosary beads and exclaimed, '*Il Papa è morto!*'

Standing on stage, I began to get frantic notes in my earpiece from the producers. Our show would begin with no audience applause. No, scrap that — there could be clapping, but no cheering. In my opening piece to camera I was to emphasise the tension not the excitement.

It struck me that no matter what we did, there was no real way to disguise the fact that the Pope was dead and we were having a dancing competition.

We sat in our studio waiting for the cue to say we were on air. On the monitor in the corner I could see a sombre reporter standing outside the Vatican doing his BBC best to convey the global significance of this tragic event. The screen went to black with the simple caption: 'Pope John Paul II, 1920–2005'. As luck would have it, the opening credits of *Strictly Dance Fever* also began with a black screen, on to which minced a white-suited me. I flicked a large power switch and the screen turned to Technicolor neon with loud upbeat dance music. I might as well have been outside the Vatican waving pom-poms and shouting, 'Boring!'

It was an early lesson in how different things were at the BBC. Every terrestrial channel is beamed into people's homes but the British Broadcasting Corporation, funded as it is by the licence fee, is held to a higher standard. The press, jealous of the corporation's resources and audience, never miss an opportunity to find fault. Back at Channel 4, high-minded journalists had hated me, but now they hated the BBC for employing me. I was more in the firing line than I had ever been before and yet I felt oddly protected by the general media hostility towards my employers. I love the BBC but as someone who is paid handsomely by them to do my job, I find I can't really champion the corporation in public, because it just sounds like the bleating of a man who knows on which side his bread is buttered. The other problem is that the BBC seems to take such pleasure in self-flagellation. Whenever it is criticised, rather than launching a stout defence, it starts another round of bloodletting, apologies and internal enquiries. Nobody is saying the place is perfect or doesn't make some pretty grave mistakes, but it is still head and shoulders above any other national broadcaster in the world. The wonderful thing about the way it is funded means it is free from the pressure of advertisers and, to a large extent, viewing figures, but it also results in everyone having the right to put the boot in. Every time there is a story about a BBC employee in the press, the comments below the article are full of people complaining about having to pay their wages. I can't speak for everyone but I know that my chat show is sold in dozens of countries abroad, meaning that it makes a sizeable contribution to the broadcaster's coffers. Someone may loathe my show but it helps fund that documentary about a lost opera by Verdi that they enjoyed so much on BBC Four.

If I ever became director general (God forbid!), I would shut the whole thing down for three months — no TV shows, radio stations, websites or live events, and then ask the nation if they had missed it. I might be very wrong, but I think most people would be very happy to cough up the 40p a day it costs them. Even if you only watch the news or listen to one show a day on the radio, that seems like extremely good value to me. Surely it means something that whenever viewers have a choice about where to watch something, be it a major sporting event, a state occasion, or something as simple as New Year's Eve celebrations, the vast majority of viewers choose the coverage on the BBC. It is our national broadcaster and I worry that if we don't treasure it now, soon it will be too late and we'll be left with a diluted version of it that pleases no one.

End of rant!

Strictly Dance Fever was very good fun to work on, and happily it wasn't a complete flop. Sadly, nor was it a hit. We did a second series but Peter Fincham, who was then the controller of BBC One, decided there would be no more. As he explained at the time, although it was a fun show it was the third most popular dancing show, trailing *Strictly Come Dancing* and ITV's *Dancing on Ice*.

So, what next for Graham at the BBC? The press had decided that I had been poached by people who had no idea what to do with me.

Looking back, I suppose the journalists had a point, but when I was going through this period I always felt busy and seemed to be working on something.

My production company had done a development deal with the BBC and we were given money to make some pilots. The first one was our attempt at a big Saturday night show. The idea was that it would be my version of *Ant and Dec's Saturday Night Takeaway*.

I'm not sure how we got it so wrong, but we did. On paper, it was a crowd-pleasing series of sketches, stunts and games, but in reality it was a pointless mess. Even on the night we shot the pilot in front of a studio audience, we sensed it would never see the light of day. We retreated to the office to lick our wounds and try again.

Our next idea couldn't have been more different. It was for a small show aimed at a late-night audience. Essentially, it was a comic look at the week's news where the three guests would author pieces, be they filmed reports, sketches or pieces to camera. The pilot went better than we'd dared hope and an unseen sketch written and performed by Mackenzie Crook from *The Office* and *Pirates of the Caribbean* remains one of my favourite things that we have ever produced. It was around the time Prince Harry had caused outrage by going to a fancy-dress party as a Nazi officer. In the sketch, Mackenzie played the owner of the fancy-dress hire shop where the prince had got his outfit, and the basic joke was that the German uniform was the least offensive costume they had in the store. I'm sure you get the idea. The sketch ended with two customers dressed as the twin towers falling over. I think you'd call it edgy.

For some reason the head of entertainment at the time, Jane Lush, was in no rush to commission it. I think she saw her job as trying to make me a mainstream family-friendly entertainer and this show, although very funny, placed me firmly in the boundary-pushing school of comedy where they had found me at Channel 4.

Eventually we took the show directly to Peter Fincham and he agreed to let us have a shot.

Having fought so hard to get the series and nearly failed, we were thrilled to have the green light. We started work on my new show, which was called *The Bigger Picture*.

The excellence of the pilot was in stark contrast to how badly the first show went. The only slot available to us was a Monday, so news either hadn't happened or it felt old already, and our guests all appeared to be too lazy or busy to take part in the production in any meaningful way. Back at Channel 4 we had made plenty of shows that stank to high heaven and we knew that you just dusted yourself off and started work on the next one, confident that it would be a lot better. But this was the BBC and the start of my brand-new series: the critics sat sharpening their pencils and set to work.

To be fair, the reviews were pretty unanimous. If I tell you that more than one of them contained the phrase 'worst show ever made', you'll have some idea of the overall tone.

The mood in the office and at the BBC was fairly dark. The only people who appeared in any way chipper were my long-time producer Jon Magnusson and myself. Firstly, we knew it was a strong format that would work eventually and secondly, it was a television series! Some journalists had gone 'Boo!', but no actual blood had been spilled or bones broken. Always remember, if you decide to come to the showbiz party the dress code is 'Thick Skin'. Our feeling was that there was no point dwelling on disaster because, according to the *Radio Times*, there was another episode of *The Bigger Picture* next Monday night.

The show eventually ran for three series before it moved to BBC Two and morphed into the chat show.

A few months later at a meeting with Peter Fincham, he mentioned a programme idea that sounded like a joke. Andrew Lloyd Webber was producing a new production of *The Sound of Music* in the West End and wanted the BBC to have an *X Factor*-style show to find someone to star in it. What elevated it in my mind from a good idea to a work of genius was the proposed programme title: *How Do You Solve a Problem Like Maria?* Here was a show that had passed my 'Would I watch it?' test with flying colours.

I immediately said that I'd love to be the host but assumed that, as with so many brilliant show ideas, it would never make it onto any television screen.

A few weeks went by and then I got a call — the 'Maria' show was still on and Andrew

Lloyd Webber would like to meet me. I realised that this wouldn't just be a lunch; this was an unofficial audition and if Andrew decided that he didn't like me then I would be left on my sofa to watch the search for a new Maria from the comfort of my own home.

The complication was that Lord Lloyd Webber and I had history. Early in 2001, Andrew's ex-wife Sarah Brightman had been a guest on my Channel 4 show. Obviously the subject of her former husband had come up and I may have said something slightly disparaging about his face. In his defence, she had announced that he had a very big willy. The audience had roared and I thought no more about it. For some reason the papers picked up on it and for a few days, the story was nearly as big as his manhood was rumoured to be. Channel 4 then got some sort of threat of legal action from the lord, so I was fairly sure Andrew was not my biggest fan.

We were to meet at a small French restaurant in Belgravia and I resolved not to order the *coq au vin*.

In the event, I needn't have worried. The lord was charm personified and so genuinely excited about the show that it was infectious. To be perfectly honest, prior to meeting Andrew, I had liked musicals but knew precious little about them. His enthusiasm is completely winning and now I love going to musicals old and new. Like a really good teacher, his passion for the subject is irresistible. The other things he adores are wine and gossip. I left the lunch having got the job and a new friend.

I enjoyed hosting the talent searches with Andrew for several reasons. They were a celebration of excellence which, it seemed to me, made them very BBC — there was no laughing at the crazy or deluded people who felt they could play the various parts; it was just genuine experts seeking truly gifted, undiscovered performers. I learnt so much and saw some really amazing performances during those shows, and it never really felt like work. I simply had the best seat in the house. One of the other things that made the experience special was working with Andrew himself. It was easy to forget, because we had such easy access to him week after week, but he is one of the greatest composers Great Britain has ever produced. This man has written songs that people will be singing long after we are all dead and this book can only be found abandoned in a dust-covered bookcase in a bed and breakfast just north of Inverness. When he critiqued the contestants we all sat up and listened because this was a man who must know what he's talking about. He's unpredictable and a bit of a producer's nightmare, but he gave the show real gravitas. In the end, we didn't just find a Maria, a Joseph, a Nancy and a Dorothy — the programme discovered dozens of brilliant singers and actors who now populate musicals on stage and film. It also introduced a whole new audience to the joys of going to see live theatre. Many people had been concerned that the shows might diminish the world of theatre but, in fact, the reverse happened: West End audiences grew and, more importantly, box office revenues increased.

★ ★ ★

Outside television, I got a rather surprising approach. The *Daily Telegraph* newspaper wondered if I had ever considered being an agony uncle. Presumably they wanted to have a face off the television in their pages and inject a bit of humour into proceedings.

They had no way of knowing, but they had inadvertently stumbled upon one of my passions. Although my own personal life is a perverse shambles, I love to dish out advice to anyone who will listen. I see a friend in tears and my face lights up. Part of my interest must come from being an outsider — the Protestant in southern Ireland, the gay boy, the loner. The key to giving advice is that feeling of being detached and empathetic at the same time.

For many years my retirement plan was to host a radio show late at night. I saw myself in a dimly lit basement studio, a dog sleeping at my feet, my voice almost whispering into the microphone: 'Hello, caller. You're on the air. How can I help you?' I'd play a selection of wrist-slitting music by Joni Mitchell and Leonard Cohen and then make my way home through the still-dark streets of London, grabbing a coffee and maybe the first edition of the newspaper from an early morning café. Lives not lived are always so appealing.

In the beginning, the letters were fairly light: problems about wedding etiquette, noisy neighbours or non-committal boyfriends. I kept my replies short and to the point, hoping to mix in a little actually helpful advice along with the jokes.

Without anyone noticing, over the last eight years the column has morphed into something very different. I still get letters from the love-starved and the outraged neighbour, but I also get many from people in genuinely dark situations who clearly have no one else to turn to. I always encourage these people to seek proper qualified assistance but then I add whatever I think might help them in the short term. Quite often I will find myself writing replies through tears.

I think the letter that changed the overall tone of the column was one I received towards the end of 2010. It struck a huge, heartbreaking chord with me and many of the readers of the *Telegraph*. Here it is, along with my reply.

Dear Graham,

My lovely mum was diagnosed in April 2010 with Lewy Body Dementia, which is Alzheimer's and Parkinson's together, plus hallucinations and occasional psychotic delusions. She has not walked since she broke her hip in a fall (physically she could, but she has forgotten how to do so) and after leaving hospital with C. diff (a serious bowel infection) which has not really cleared, she is now bedridden, cannot lift her head from the pillow and weighs less than 4 stone. Her skin is beginning to break down and she eats a few teaspoons of puréed food once a day. She cries a lot but cannot tell me what is wrong as her vocabulary is now down to half a dozen words.

I cannot accept what has happened. I work four days a week and am married with two young boys and I go to the nursing home every day, sometimes twice. I realise I cannot make her any better but I am just so angry that her life has come to this. My brother cannot cope with this either. He rarely visits and leaves the financial side to me.

My husband is not particularly supportive but doesn't moan about me going to the nursing home all the time. He can't understand why I am so emotional about the whole thing. His opinion is that it's happened; deal with it.

I know he is right but I don't know how to. My doctor has offered medication but I don't see the point, as it can't change anything. I am probably exhausted but then I look at my mum and think, 'What have I got to complain about?'

The sad thing is that if she was a pet I would be prosecuted for keeping her alive in such a pitiful state. Her doctors think she has weeks, possibly days to live but can't really say. I have good friends to talk to but no one really gets it, plus I'm aware that it's depressing for others to listen to. I want her to die. I want her to live. I don't know what to do. Please help.

NS, South-East London

Dear NS,

These days are as dark as they will ever be. Your mum — your lovely mum — the woman who fed and cared for you, the arms that held you to make you believe everything would be all right, now lies in a bed like a bird that has fallen from its nest. Of course you want to howl at the sky at the injustice of it all. No one deserves the fate that has befallen your mother.

The good news is that soon it will all be over and you can look at yourself in the mirror knowing that you were a good daughter who did everything there was to be done. Of course you don't want to say goodbye but equally no one could wish this woman to linger long in her current state.

Don't be too hard on your husband or friends. This is the worst bit. Soon there will be a funeral and everyone will know how to act around you again. We all understand death and mourning but what you are going through at the moment is, in a way, much worse and harder to understand.

There is no wrong way to feel right now. Be furious. Be heartbroken. Be glad she's gone. Be lonely. It seems so unlikely, but time will heal all of this and then you and your brother and the rest of your family and friends can remember the woman your mother really was.

Don't let this horrible end rob you of the amazing story that went before.

It is a privilege to get such letters full of raw pain and despair, and yet I wonder what effect it has on the writers. From having absolutely no one to turn to, suddenly your private anguish is laid bare in such a public forum. Clearly for some people that is part of the appeal or columns like this wouldn't have lasted. Perhaps it is simply the act of putting the problem down on paper that helps the writer cope, even before anyone else has given their advice. I know in my own life when I'm upset by something so much that I can't even sleep, if I just mention it to another person, it suddenly feels like it's not the end of the world. Words don't just communicate the dilemma; they define it and turn it into a fixed target ready to be dealt with.

I do sometimes wonder why readers enjoy such columns. Is it really as simple as rejoicing in the misery of others? That feeling that your own life isn't as awful as you thought because here are people who are in straits that are much more dire? That may indeed be part of the appeal but I also think it's about asking yourself, 'What would I do?' and comparing your answer to the reply from the agony aunt or uncle.

The one thing I'm certain of is that I'm incapable of applying to myself any of the advice I dish out so freely. Often I blush as I reply to people who are in a similar situation to one I've experienced and I know I failed to do any of the sensible, sane things that I am now suggesting to a stranger. Even afterwards I can't be certain I wouldn't just repeat my same old mistakes. When it comes to matters of the heart, it seems that knowledge is not power. Physician, heal thyself.

★ ★ ★

Back in the shallow world of bright lights and television cameras, I found myself at the whim of various commissioners and executives. *The Bigger Picture* had slowly become much more of a chat show. Yes, it still had topical material, but equally it was very easy for a celebrity to use it as a way of promoting a film or a book. After Channel 4, I had resisted the idea of immediately doing another chat show. Why move to the BBC if I was just going to replicate what I had already been doing? Now it appeared that, despite my best intentions, I was once more the host of a chat show.

BBC One already had *Friday Night with Jonathan Ross* but the controller of BBC Two, Roly Keating, was happy to offer us a new home.

In the spring of 2007 we launched *The Graham Norton Show*.

Some aspects we kept from *The Bigger Picture*. Having all the guests on at the same time had worked well, as did introducing them en masse rather than giving each guest a protracted introduction. Initially, we also tried to keep some sort of news agenda going, picking up from stories of the week to break up the chat, but that was soon abandoned in favour of finding items that related more directly to the guests. It doesn't take a genius to notice that most people, especially egocentric stars, are much happier talking about themselves rather than new laws to try and curb binge drinking.

I really enjoy the process of starting a new show. Talking with the set designer, working on a title sequence and choosing music — I can't do any of those jobs but that doesn't stop me getting very involved along the way. Having your name in the title should mean that you can stand behind every aspect of the show. Hopefully I'm open to other people's ideas and expertise but, ultimately, I have to feel like I own it.

The show played on Thursday evenings and people seemed to like it. We also noticed that we were reaping the rewards of having done a chat show for so many years, because our guest list was much more impressive than one would expect for a fledgling show on the second channel.

Our success and mainstream appeal soon meant that BBC One, despite having Jonathan's show, started sniffing around. Jay Hunt was the new controller and she was busy cherry-picking shows from the sister channel. It was decided that we would move back to BBC One and return to our previous slot of Monday nights.

The press immediately started pitting our show against Jonathan Ross's. For some reason, chat-show wars always make good headlines but in reality, the rivalry is much exaggerated. Booking guests is never easy and even if you had the only chat show on television, it would still be extremely difficult to coax the stars out of their hotel rooms and off their red carpets to sit in front of an audience on your sofa.

As a way of welcoming my show to the channel and dispelling any rumours of animosity, Jonathan asked me to appear on his as a guest and I was happy to do so. I am a big fan of Jonathan Ross and always watch his shows. He is extremely gifted at what he does, which is why I took no pleasure at all in what happened next.

Luck is a factor in any career, be it good or bad. It turned out that Jonathan Ross's very bad luck would become my good fortune. Of course you may be reading this and thinking to yourself that what happened to Jonathan was nothing to do with luck, that the prank calls he and Russell Brand made to the actor Andrew Sachs that led to his suspension were simply an error of judgement. Of course you'd be right, but when you are working at the risqué edge of comedy that Jonathan and Russell inhabit, it is very important to be surrounded by people who remind you of the line and pull you back. It was a pre-recorded show that was played in a late-night slot on Radio 2. I find it impossible to believe that any producer, no matter how inexperienced, would have played out those phone calls without running them past someone. The bad language alone would have needed to be cleared, never mind the actual content.

In the end, what caused Jonathan's downfall was the fact that it was a quiet news time between Obama's election and his inauguration; and, most of all, his much-publicised £18-million-pound deal with the BBC.

The artificially inflated sense of outrage forced the BBC to act. Russell Brand had already resigned, leaving Jonathan to be the fall guy. The punishment might have been a twelve-week suspension but after that it was inevitable the corporation and Jonathan would part ways. I think every other comic and presenter working for the BBC looked on with a deep sense of 'There but for the grace of God . . . '

It wasn't long till the ripples of the controversy reached my career. I have always adored the Eurovision Song Contest and made no secret of the fact that I would have loved to take over doing the commentary should the great Sir Terry Wogan ever decide to relinquish the role. My agent, Melanie, had mentioned this on more than one occasion to the various heads of entertainment and BBC One controllers, but she had always received a fairly lukewarm response to her suggestion: 'We'll certainly keep him in mind,' was about the best that she could muster from the powers that be. Now, we heard a rumour.

I have no idea if it was true and I've never asked the people involved, but whispers suggested that Jonathan Ross had staked a claim on the job and I have to admit that giving him the role made sense. He was the biggest entertainment star they had at the time and he would have been in stark contrast to the previous occupier of the position.

I'm sure Sir Terry was oblivious to such machinations when he announced his retirement from Eurovision in early December 2008, but with Jonathan still embroiled in the phone-call scandal, the job was offered to me. I didn't hesitate.

My agent was at pains to tell me that I had always been the first choice for the job. Maybe she's right but I'm not so sure. As it happens, I don't really care, as I get to do the job and I love it.

Even though I was a replacement on Eurovision, I never felt like I was stepping into a dead man's shoes — Sir Terry had walked away of his own free will. I may still be entranced by the ridiculous costumes, eccentric staging and controversial voting, but after thirty-five years I imagine its appeal might wear a little thin.

What made taking over easier was that Terry was so gracious. In the press he gave me his blessing, and in private he called to wish me luck and offer some sage advice: 'Don't have a drink before song seven.'

★　★　★

My first Eurovision Song Contest was in Moscow, which may well be Russian for 'shithole'. It really is a grim city and the population seem to agree as they wend their depressed, unfriendly way through its traffic-filled streets. Happily, I was reunited with Andrew Lloyd Webber because he had composed our song that year, along with the legendary songwriter, Diane Warren.

In light of all the budgetary concerns at the BBC I was pleasantly surprised when I saw my hotel room in Moscow. It was a plush suite with over-stuffed sofas and champagne in a bucket. How lovely! I then noticed the message scrolling across the television screen: 'Welcome, Lord Graham Norton.' Clearly there had been some confusion with the booking. I had visions of Andrew in his single room staring out at a rusty fire escape clutching a small packet of dry biscuits.

Jade, who later became a Sugababe, did the

267

singing honours that year. Although most people think the UK always do badly, in 2009 we finished a very respectable fifth.

Despite all the talk of rigged voting and Eastern bloc bias, the very next year Germany triumphed in the contest, which to me indicates that all bets are off. In 2014, Conchita brought the Eurovision home to Austria for the first time since 1966. When the people of Europe decided that a bearded man in a flowing gown, singing a song about pride and reinvention, was a worthy winner, I fell in love with the competition a little more and, for a few brief moments, felt optimistic about the future of Europe. It is important to remember that not all governments actually represent their people. As the confetti fell and Conchita reprised her winning song, the commentators emerged from their small rabbit-hutch commentary booths and quite a few of them were in tears. I was one of them.

★ ★ ★

2010 had hardly begun when the news broke: Jonathan Ross would not be renewing his contract with the BBC. My phone immediately started ringing with friends, agents and producers all wondering what it meant for our show. Would we get the now-vacant Friday-night slot?

It was fun to speculate but not for long — a statement was released by Jay Hunt saying we would not be moving. Oh. It did seem like an odd decision given how well we were doing in the graveyard shift on a Monday, but the powers that be, we surmised, must have some other plan. Fair enough.

The other prime slot that had now become free was Saturday mornings on BBC Radio 2. I loved Jonathan on the radio and if I'm being perfectly honest, I thought it was better than his TV show. Knowing how loyal listeners can be I had no desire to take over. I felt very strongly that whoever came next in that slot would fail spectacularly.

Typically, having been told I couldn't have the Friday night that I felt confident the show could fill, I got the call to say that Bob Shennan, the controller of Radio 2, was offering me the Saturday mornings. My agent seemed keen. I explained my misgivings and hoped that Bob would understand. I stressed what a big fan I was of the station, but I just didn't feel up to the challenge.

Despite everything, I got another call saying that Bob would still like to meet. What was the point? I'm not a big lover of meetings at the best of times and this one just seemed like a waste of everyone's time. 'Please?' My agent rarely insists or tries to change my mind, so since it meant so much to her, I reluctantly agreed.

Some people are much better face-to-face than they are on the phone and that is clearly the case with Bob Shennan. I can't even remember what he said but I know I walked out of his office fairly convinced that I would be a moron to turn down the opportunity to have my own show on Radio 2, especially in such a prime slot. The main thrust of his argument was that chances like this don't come along very often.

A TV career can be quite precarious and having just been very publicly snubbed by the controller of BBC One, I was more aware of this than ever. The future of my television show did not look very bright. Radio, on the other hand, was much more stable and provided longevity, along with an enormous audience that means you maintain a presence long after other outlets have washed their hands of you.

Given how much I adore doing the radio show, I'm incredulous that I came so close to walking away. As we begin our fifth year, the audiences are at an all-time high and we even got some sort of bronze award that in the right light can look like gold. I love the spontaneity of the show. Yes, there is a great deal of production put into the programme by my producer Malcolm Prince and his assistant Paul Mann, but that means I can show up at 9.15 and leave just after 1 p.m. It is in stark contrast to the television show, which takes days to look like nobody cares.

Interviewing one of my guests on the radio, I am handed an A4 piece of paper with some biographical facts, which I read during the record before we start our chat. If it goes well, wonderful; if it is a little stilted, let's play some more music. For the television show, however, the researchers provide a twenty-page document on each guest and almost two days is spent weaving the questions and anecdotes together for the studio recording. In my opinion, doing that amount of preparation for the radio show would make it sound less fun for the listeners and render a three-hour show unproduceable. Such an approach is completely unrelated to any rumours you may have heard about my laziness. Truly.

One of my greatest pleasures is the interaction with the listeners who email and text the show. They seem like a genuinely lovely bunch and it is an honour to be part of their weekly routine. When Maria McErlane and I ask people to help with the problems that have been sent in for the feature called 'Grill Graham', I'm confident that their responses will be sympathetic, funny and to the point. Behind the scenes, the station also has a family feel, particularly on a Saturday morning when it is just a skeleton crew. Bobbie Pryor knows a great deal about travel, though her knowledge of popular culture suggests that she may have been raised by wolves. The legend that is Tony Blackburn always pops into our studio to say hello, or at least that's his story — the truth is he just wants to eat some of our extensive supply of biscuits. Most Saturday mornings find me feeling at best tired and at worst hung-over, so I tend to consume more sugar and caffeine during those three hours than I do for the rest of the week.

I'm sure events were slightly spaced out but in my memory it feels like I had just hung up the phone after accepting the radio show, when it rang again with the news that Jay Hunt had changed her mind and was now going to move the chat show to Friday. I knew this was obviously great news for the show, but I hated that it now gave the impression that I was roaming the corridors of the BBC trying to hoover up all of Jonathan's jobs.

The added complication was that we didn't know when we would be moving to the Friday slot. It was explained to me that the executives were trying to protect our show, this time by giving us as much distance as possible from the end of Jonathan's series. This was very lovely of them but in the meantime we had no idea when to book the studios or guests for. By all means protect us, but try not to have that end up with us filming the show in a Scout hut in Eastbourne interviewing a man who can sculpt Biblical characters using old plastic bags! It was long past the eleventh hour when we were finally greenlit for 22 October.

Despite all our concerns about comparisons to Jonathan Ross on both television and radio, the audiences seemed to have remarkably short memories. In the event, people are only concerned about the quality of what they are actually watching or listening to, not what used to be broadcast in those slots. It was a harsh reminder that no one is irreplaceable and that when I stop doing the shows, the audience will move on just as quickly. The shallow nature of the work I do means that more people stop me in the street when the show is being aired — by the end of the summer, during our hiatus, I notice a real drop in the number of people nudging each other in the supermarket or beeping their car horns when I'm out with the dogs. Out of sight really does seem to mean out of mind.

The Friday-night slot might have been new but we were very clear that we would be doing the same old show. We rejected the offer of an hour in favour of our usual forty-five minutes. In my view, a chat show without any commercial breaks is long enough with that running time. True, there are shows when we wish they could go on for longer, but I still think there are more shows when we are very glad we aren't trying to fill another fifteen minutes.

Since we started doing chat shows back when we were on Channel 4, we have always tried to include some sort of audience interaction. In the beginning it was the 'Stand up, sit down' section where we used a game to seek out audience stories. We still do a similar thing except now it is at the end of the show and members of the public try to tell their stories without being flipped out of a big red chair. Jon Magnusson came up with the idea the first time Ronnie Corbett was a guest on the show. Based on the long stories he would tell on *The Two Ronnies*, the idea was to see how members of the public would fare telling their own favourite anecdotes — if we got bored, we would simply pull a lever and the storyteller would be ejected into oblivion. It was only meant to be a one-off but the special manufacture of the chair had proved more expensive than anyone had expected so we were trying to think of other ways to use it. In 2009, when we came back in the autumn, Jon explained his idea. Each show would end with a feature called 'That's all we've got time for . . . ' Essentially, it was a way to use the audience and give viewers a reason to stay tuned after the musical performances. It was an experiment. That night Ozzy and Sharon Osbourne sat alongside Olivia Newton-John and watched with glee as members of the public got flipped so that only their legs remained to wave goodbye. Over 150 shows later we're still doing it, and it remains one of my favourite parts of the show. Russell Crowe claims it is the only reason he comes on, while Tom Cruise refuses to touch the lever.

Guests. A chat show, no matter how great its comedy segments and production may be, is ultimately judged by the size of the stars gracing its couch. When I think back to the days when our booker would head down to London's media hang-out, the Groucho Club, with a bag of cash hoping to entice someone we had heard of to do our show, it is amazing to think of the stars we are now playing host to. Late 2013 and Robert De Niro, Harrison Ford, Sir Paul McCartney, Dame Judi Dench, Sir Elton John, Cher and Lady Gaga all came to chat within a month. Of course, being very famous gets an audience extremely excited but it is no guarantee of chat-show gold. Harrison Ford or Robert De Niro will never represent their country at the Chatting Olympics but our challenge is to put them on the couch with people they will enjoy so that they reveal themselves not through their own stories, but in how they react to the anecdotes and revelations of others.

For me, as the host, it takes a lot of pressure off knowing that I don't have to try and get blood from a stone — it doesn't matter what you do or who you are, there are certain people who, when you see you are going to have to sit next to them at the dinner party or in the pub, your heart sinks. Nothing can save you. There is a very famous episode of the *David Letterman Show* where Dave was forced by De Niro's monosyllabic answers to resort to reading aloud the names of De Niro's movies to an applauding audience. That's tough. Equally, being a huge celebrity doesn't necessarily mean you will be too grand to muck about and have fun. Tom Hanks, Will Smith, Glenn Close and Dustin Hoffman are clowns at heart and come alive in front of 600 people. When we had *The Fresh Prince of Bel-Air* reunion, complete with the dance, the audience roared like nothing I have ever heard before. I felt like Oprah when she gave everyone a car.

My favourite shows are the ones that take me by surprise. Putting people side by side on the couch is like conducting an experiment in chemistry, where you've no idea how the various elements will react. Of course we plan it and hope for the best but on the night there is always a slight sense of dread as you wait to discover the results of that particular experiment. No one could have predicted what would happen when the actress Miriam Margolyes met Will.i.am from the Black Eyed Peas. Their worlds are so different and Miriam's candour so extreme that it might have been socially awkward or even offensive, but what we saw was the blossoming of a wonderful rapport and friendship. When Lady Gaga met *EastEnders*' June Brown, a similar thing happened. The author and filmmaker John Waters still waxes lyrical about meeting Justin Bieber. One of my favourite shows of recent times had Matt Damon, Bill Murray and *Downton Abbey*'s Hugh Bonneville. They were on to promote a movie called *The Monuments Men*, directed by George Clooney. Originally we had planned a whole show that included another star of the movie, the French Oscar-winner, Jean Dujardin. The day before filming, following an unhappy time on another show in Italy, he pulled out. The publicists were very apologetic but told us that there was a possibility Bill Murray might

276

step in to replace him.

I like working against deadlines, but under-prepared shows rarely turn out that well. But this was different. The three men clearly relished being in each other's company and the free-flowing conversation that resulted was some of the best we've ever had. At one point Matt Damon was moved to declare that it was the most fun he had ever had on a chat show. If I were clever enough to know how, I'd have that clip as the ring tone on my phone!

Happily, having all the guests on at the same time usually works for everybody. If a guest tells a story that doesn't go well, they don't need to worry because later on they will get another chance to shine. If someone is being a tad dull, I can involve the other guests to cheer things up. So far we have been really lucky with the chemistry that has been produced on the couch. I can only recall a few occasions when it was less than ideal. Alex Kingston was clearly not a big fan of Rob Lowe and called him out on the show for the way he was talking about some of his former conquests. As if to prove her point, he said something about her playing a nurse on *ER*. No, Rob, Alex played a doctor. Women can do that. Another battle of the sexes involved Lord Alan Sugar and the comedian and writer Pamela Stephenson. She was talking about her work as a therapist and Lord Sugar didn't feel the need to sweeten his opinion when he told her she was a quack that had bought her qualifications. Awkward.

The unnamed guest at the table that can

sometimes cause problems is booze. We encourage the guests to have a drink on set with them because as we all know from life, it can help people relax and oil the wheels of conversation, but sometimes the overly relaxed wheels can come off. I'm not sure the beautiful actress Jessica Biel will ever want to share a couch with Mickey Rourke and his best friend Jack Daniel's ever again. I don't know how it happened but at one point he had her in handcuffs, which I feel guests on a chat show should never have to deal with. The most extreme case of over-indulgence was undoubtedly the episode we taped with Mark Wahlberg, Sarah Silverman and Michael Fassbender. I don't know what happened backstage but I suspect Mr Wahlberg may have had more than the two glasses of red wine he consumed on the show. It began pleasantly enough when he was talking about his movie but then it was as if a curtain was lowered and the lights went out. Happily I got the impression that Sarah and Michael had been around their fair share of drunk people so they both coped brilliantly. At one point Mark clambered on my knee and started to pinch my nipples. As I tried to get him back on the couch I thought about my younger self and how much I had fancied this man. There was an Annie Leibovitz photograph in *Vanity Fair* where a small dog was pulling off Mark's famous underwear. That image had kept me warm on many a night, but now here I was trying to stop him manhandling me. My younger self's head would have exploded. At one point I noticed that Michael Fassbender was managing to tell a story without interruption. Odd. I glanced over at Mark Wahlberg. He was asleep. Everyone's a critic.

The chat show in its various forms has made all my dreams come true and opened doors to worlds I never knew existed. I owe it everything and still after all these years enjoy it as much as I ever have, if not more. The question then is, 'When will it stop?' Retirement seems like such an odd word to apply to myself because I still feel so full of energy and enthusiasm, but at the same time I have no desire to be a Bruce Forsyth or Des O'Connor. I love working but I also want some time to enjoy my life without the constraints and pressures that come with my job. The secret is to get bored of the show before the audience does, and I'm not there yet, but knowing where to stop the story to ensure a happy ending is the toughest job of all. I've just signed a contract to stay with the BBC for another three years so I suppose the answer to the question of stopping is, 'Sometime after that.' In a career that had so many false starts and years of struggle before it really began, it will be hard to say goodbye. It almost feels like being ungrateful.

The other thing to consider is that you're not just leaving behind an income stream and public recognition — the people I work with are like my family, but with that special bond that you only get from making a show together. In the end I'm sure it isn't the applause I would miss, it would be the easy banter that comes with sharing triumphs and failures.

This story came close to ending on my fiftieth birthday. That day — 4 April 2013 — fell on a Thursday so I found myself taping the first show of the new season on it. In the audience were some friends who were going out with me after the recording to raise a glass before the actual big bash that was planned for the Saturday.

For this particular episode there was an electric atmosphere in the studio that had nothing to do with my half-century and everything to do with the man waiting backstage: Tom Cruise. This was to be his second appearance on the show and I was really looking forward to it.

I have met a great number of famous people over the years but Tom Cruise is one of the very few to actually dazzle me with their star quality. He makes you feel hypnotised by his gaze and all my preconceptions about the man melted away. He's one of the very few stars who doesn't just shine his light on the host. Everyone who met him backstage felt exactly the same as he shook hands and remembered each name, no matter what their job description. Humble and presidential at the same time, it may be an act, but if so, it's the best I've ever seen.

Each week on the show, there is a little teaser about the guests that precedes the opening title sequence. The term we use for it is something we learnt working in America: a 'cold open'. That night we were making a reference to Tom in *Mission Impossible* so I was suspended on wires above the audience. We had rehearsed the sequence in the afternoon and a special rigging company had been hired along with a stunt co-ordinator. It seemed a little like overkill when all we were really doing was tying a rapidly aging homosexual to a rope and lifting him up and down. On the night it went very smoothly and afterwards I stood on the stairs that run through the middle of the audience while the team of experts removed the various bits of harness. Clearly one member of the team was less than expert and dropped the ball — the 'ball' being a large metal bar that had been holding the whole flying apparatus in the lighting rig.

It could have come hurtling down and hit the floor with a resounding *clang* but as luck would have it, the whole thing landed on my head.

There were two extraordinary sounds. The first was a sickening *crack* that echoed out from my skull to fill the whole studio, and the second was 600 people gasping and holding their breath. I waited a moment. Was I going to pass out? Would my eyes cloud over with the blood haemorrhaging from my brain? Was this how it all ended?

In the event I just got a bad headache, the show went on, and we scratched the number for that rigging company out of our book of contacts. Afterwards, the phrase I heard most often wasn't 'Happy Birthday' but 'You could have died!' Later that night, lying in bed, I thought about how close I had come to checking out at fifty, the smiling faces of friends in the audience; the biggest movie star in the world on the couch. It was a very odd thing to lie staring up at a dark ceiling and acknowledge that I would have died happy, but I have to admit it was a very good feeling, too.

8

Things I Love to Hate

A whole book devoted to the things that I love does seem unacceptably upbeat. This section aims to redress the balance a little. I am generally quite a cheerful person, but certain things can unleash my inner Victor Meldrew.

Loud sneezing

You *can* help it. I understand that sometimes people sneeze and they are often taken by surprise, but there is no need to turn it into an impression of the midday gun in Hong Kong. If you are *that* desperate for attention, why not develop a personality and a sense of humour?

Local news

Maybe this is just something I feel because I live in London, but surely if an event is really news, it will be on that other programme called *The News*? Should there be a local incident that is going to impact on me then I imagine I can look out of my window and see what's going on. I have no interest in the spate of graffiti in Newham or the birth of some ducklings on a pond behind the printing works near that other place I never go.

Drunk people

Hypocrite? Moi? I know this is a little rich coming from this particular boozehound but I'm only referring to certain sorts of drunk people. Obviously I remain as cute as a kitten as I slip in my own vomit, explaining at the top of my voice to no one in particular why *E.T.* is the greatest film ever made, but somehow there are members of the human race who can become a tad annoying when alcohol is added. Specifically there is a noise that large groups of pissed-up women make that I credit with making me gay.

Guilty pleasures

The phrase is used by so many people and it makes my blood boil. Unless your pleasure is bear-baiting or watching snuff movies, then save your guilt for something that deserves it. Listening to S Club 7 singing 'Reach' while you dance around your kitchen might be embarrassing but it is not worth feeling guilty about. This is related to when I worked in restaurants and asked people if they wanted dessert. 'Oh, I really shouldn't!' they would cry as if I'd asked them to kill their first-born rather than offered them a slice of cake. Keep some perspective, please!

Farce

I can admire it. I can appreciate the skill involved. What I can't do is enjoy it. As the case of mistaken identity escalates the people around me are howling with laughter but I'm just stressed. Movies like *Planes, Trains and Automobiles* or John Cleese's *Clockwise* make me grind my teeth. I just want to step in and yell, 'Stop!' There is never any real need for the situation to continue. Although not pure farce, *Curb Your Enthusiasm* also falls into this runaway train of embarrassment. It is a work of genius with brilliant writing and performances, but I just want someone to explain the situation and make it stop. My approach would lead to a lot of very short, unfunny plays and movies, but I'd enjoy them more that way.

Vox pops

I don't care what you think. If the government is bringing in new tax legislation, then please interview a financial expert who can explain the ramifications for the economy and people's take-home pay; do not ask a man loitering outside Clinton Cards what he thinks. The very fact that someone had so little going on in their lives that they agreed to talk to a camera crew immediately negates their opinion in my view. But what do you think?

Grapefruit

Got very sick after eating it when I was a child. 'Nuff said.

Beach holidays

If my dogs are involved then I love the beach, but if the aim is to lie down and sunbathe then get me to a swimming pool. Sand is just dirt that has been given a makeover — I don't want it on me, in my book or sprinkled on my food like gritty, tasteless seasoning. Added to this, preparing for swimming at the beach is invariably an undignified affair: standing on one leg, wrestling with a towel and your togs like a drunk Harry Houdini and then afterwards trying to put on clothes that want to stick to every part of your body apart from where you would like them to be.

Self-help

Now I am all in favour of self-improvement. Learn how to make an authentic curry. Dazzle me with your command of the French language. Lose weight, build muscle, don't be afraid to change and evolve. What you shouldn't do is spend hours of your life and a great deal of cash getting ready for some life that you won't start living until you are completely ready. What are you waiting for? If life is a party it has started already and it turns out it's a 'come as you are' affair. The time you spent preparing yourself for the challenges of living are big chunks of life you will never get back. Skills may be contained in books, but wisdom is acquired from experience and mistakes. I intend to write a whole book about this. I hope you like it.

Sharing

The waiter approaches the table and asks, 'Are you familiar with the concept of our menu?' and a chill creeps across my skin. Invariably they go on to explain that it is a sharing menu with several small dishes. For two people they suggest five plates. When someone feels the need to elaborate on how to order food off a menu I always know that by the end of the evening I will be over-charged and underfed. Maybe it is because of the Irish famine but I'm always very territorial about my dinner. I don't mind sharing my lunch or a starter but my main course has been carefully selected to get me through to breakfast without starving to death. Hands off.

Prolonged celebrations

Let's be clear. I am thrilled that you are getting married, having a birthday or marking an anniversary, but please remember why it is called 'your special day'. If you want your friends to come to your wedding, isn't it just good manners to get married where the majority of your friends live? I've been to quite a few weddings and have learned what to expect. The happy couple look happy, the chicken looks dry, and the best man looks terrified. Do I really need to get on a plane to see that? It seems that more and more couples are confusing the wedding with the honeymoon. Staring at your sweaty faces with nothing to say for two weeks is your job — the guests get to go home. I wonder how many people have found themselves unable to afford to get married because of the fortunes they have shelled out travelling the globe to see other people getting hitched? Special day, people, special day.

Camera phones

Actually, I have nothing against camera phones as such — it is the people who attempt to use them that make me want to rip them out of their hands and stamp on them like a cowboy trying to put out a fire. To begin with, I thought they were an improvement on the old-fashioned habit of asking for an autograph. Unless I am in a serious rush I always sign whatever is thrust in front of me but always question why anyone would want it. Usually it involves a scrap of paper or the back of a magazine that before the night is out will have been lost or, if it's kept, the identity of the mystery scribe will have been long forgotten. Sometimes people are very organised, with multiple photographs and autograph books. The received wisdom amongst celebrities is that people are somehow making money out of the signatures. One glance at the hunched, anorak-covered shoulders and lank, greasy hair suggests that their income stream isn't exactly rivalling that of Bill Gates. If they want to waste their lives standing in the rain outside Radio 2 or reaching through the railings of London Television Studios like the living dead, then I say good luck to them. Nothing, in fact, will beat an experience I had eating in a very posh London restaurant with my friend Maria. Both of our fathers were suffering with Parkinson's disease and while talking about their condition we had both started to cry. Unbelievably, that is when a man thought it would be a good time to drag his wife over to the table and ask me to sign her tits. I did.

The arrival of camera phones made more sense to me than autographs. It is quite nice to have a photograph to commemorate the moment you met a favourite celebrity — I have a few dotted around my house. The problem is that nobody appears to know how to use them. The seconds spent scrawling a name on a piece of paper have been replaced by several minutes as people take pictures of their own eye or discover that they are in fact videoing you. Helpful people step in: 'Would you like me to take it for you?' Invariably these helpful citizens then behave as if they have been offered a ticking bomb to defuse. You offered! I don't interrupt brain surgeons and suggest I lend a helping hand because I know that I have no idea how to operate. If you ask me for a photo I will try and be nice — unless it's at the gym, fuck you very much — but please bear in mind other things that might be going on in my day. If you are the umpteenth person to ask, my smile won't be quite as wide, or if Bailey the labradoodle has just vomited I may seem distracted. And if I'm discussing the death of a loved one, I might just be in tears. Say cheese!

Tweets from animals

Surely this requires no explanation.

The internet

Well, of course I don't really hate the internet; I just hate what it does to me. Clearly it is an extraordinary research tool and source of news, so why then do I find myself spending hours sitting in front of a computer screen watching videos of a man who can slice up a cabbage to look like a map of the world, or a six-year-old dancer who blew the judges away on *India's Got Talent*? Sometimes it can fool you into thinking it matters. When I end up in floods of tears watching Bruno Mars singing to a blind girl, it feels like time well spent but in reality my time would have been more wisely used folding laundry, trimming nose hair or, in fact, doing almost anything else apart from watching the pocket-sized pop star tug at my heart strings. Equally, the various social media sites can be a great way of keeping in touch with out-of-the-way friends but in practice I spend my time scrolling through hundreds of holiday snaps of people I don't really know holding pints of lager and wrapping sunburnt arms around more people I don't know. I actually become impatient when the photographs don't load fast enough because, yet again, some weird part of my brain has convinced me that this is time well spent and that seeing every identical drunken image is somehow important.

Part of the problem is surely that we can now surf the web wherever we are. There is no escape. On safari in Tanzania, I could look out of the window at gazelles drinking from a watering hole, but in my room the presence of wi-fi meant I was actually looking at pictures of Lady Gaga leaving a bar in New York. We used to be safe on planes — a refuge from emails and Facebook status updates — but now airlines are proudly announcing the availability of internet on board. Does the web really need to be worldwide? It used to feel like something that magically connected us to every corner of the globe but increasingly the web feels like a trap.

For ever

For ever isn't a long, long time. It's a lie. Who came up with this concept that's designed to torture and disappoint us? Nothing lasts for ever and that's just the way things should be. As I write this, Bailey the labradoodle is doing his impression of a giant's wig that has been thrown into a corner of the room. He's crying about something. I don't know what, but I do know he'll stop when he realises I'm ignoring him. It'll pass. And, all too soon, I'll be crying but I'll know why — the giant's wig won't be stuffed in the corner any more. Of course if I was asked if I wanted Bailey to live for ever I would say yes, but in reality knowing that he will leave me makes my time with him more precious, the love bittersweet. We enjoy the party because we know there will come a time when the music will be switched off and the lights switched on. We allow ourselves to sob at the funeral because we know it's not for ever. One of the great joys of life is knowing that things change. Relish the happy times; endure the sad. For ever is a pointless fantasy. Everything comes to an end — the good, the bad and now, it seems, this book.

Acknowledgements

Nearly all of my fantasies have become a reality but I have started to make my peace with the fact that I may never get to make my Oscar acceptance speech, so I'm using this bit of the book to thank the many people who have helped get me this far in my life, my career and my book.

It is unbearably maudlin, but I must begin by thanking my family. Being my mother or sister isn't easy. For the first thirty years of my life they worried that I would end up dead in a gutter, and for the last twenty years they've endured stares in the supermarket and visits from unwelcome journalists. Thank you so much for your patience during both phases. I forbade my mother from reading my last book but I think she can read this one, after I've torn out a few pages.

Melanie Rockcliffe at Troika is the sort of agent who thinks you are better than you actually are, but then miraculously her blind faith in you is rewarded. I'm so pleased that in her own life she has been so well rewarded with Mark and the miracle that is Finley.

Dylan Hearn also works at Troika and, along with Will Darlow, guides me through my career choices, complicated calendar and my own stupidity.

At So Television, Graham Stuart drives the car while the rest of us are the kids going nuts on the back seat. Jon Magnusson makes me so much better than I am and Tony Jordan brings all the stars to the yard. I want to name everyone at So but I feel this thank-you section will get out of hand. I raise a glass to the rest of the team who invest more of their heart, soul, sweat and tears than any television programme deserves. We've worked together for so long it is like being part of a family and, like any family, we have good times as well as bad. Now our family has grown. Welcome to the world, Mamie Magnusson.

Charlotte Moore and Mark Linsey are the people who think our show is fit for BBC One and we do our best not to let them down too often. Tony Hall is the director general of the BBC. He has lovely hair.

At Radio 2, big thanks to Bob Shennan and Lewis Carnie for bringing me on board and endless gratitude for the endless hard work and organisational skills of Malcolm Prince and Paul Mann for keeping me on board and on air. Paul, apparently a child himself, is now daddy to Oliver. Look, baby Oliver, your name is in a book!

Enormous thanks to everyone at Hodder for making this book a reality. Rowena Webb for getting me on board, Alasdair Oliver and Kate

Brunt for making it look so very stylish. A huge thank you to the effortlessly talented Clym Evernden for the illustrations. Lucy Hale, Vickie Boff and Veronique Norton for letting the world know about the book in various genius ways. Claudette Morris for getting it into print. Liz Caraffi for her support and a special mention to Hannah Black for her supreme patience. She encouraged me to keep on writing without ever uttering the phrase, 'Hurry the fuck up!'

Friends. Too many friends to list! I love them all. I thought that by the time I'd reached fifty I would have made all my friends and I would no longer be adding names. It is an unexpected joy that the list keeps growing. Here's to friends old and new.

Kristian made it into the acknowledgements of the hardback edition of my last book but was removed from the paperback. Now here he is again. Kristian has asked me to point out that he is much older and wiser now and would make someone a wonderful boyfriend.

Mark Wright, who loves Bailey and Madge when I'm not available to do it myself. The three of us say thanks.

Thank you to the incomparable Becky Wales. There doesn't appear to be a single thing she can't do and without her my life would be an utter shambles. I'm sure there are many occasions when she just wants to throw a stapler at my head but she always manages to keep a smile on her face. The biggest smile of all was saved for the day she married Ben. Congratulations!

The final thanks must go to you, the reader. Whether you received this book as a gift, bought it yourself, or simply shoplifted it in error, thanks for being interested enough to open its covers. If you watch or listen to any of my shows, thanks for that as well. None of what I do actually matters, but without an audience it really would be pointless.

We do hope that you have enjoyed reading this large print book.

Did you know that all of our titles are available for purchase?

We publish a wide range of high quality large print books including:
Romances, Mysteries, Classics
General Fiction
Non Fiction and Westerns

Special interest titles available in large print are:
The Little Oxford Dictionary
Music Book
Song Book
Hymn Book
Service Book

Also available from us courtesy of Oxford University Press:
Young Readers' Dictionary
(large print edition)
Young Readers' Thesaurus
(large print edition)

For further information or a free brochure, please contact us at:
Ulverscroft Large Print Books Ltd.,
The Green, Bradgate Road, Anstey,
Leicester, LE7 7FU, England.
Tel: **(00 44) 0116 236 4325**
Fax: **(00 44) 0116 234 0205**

IN THE FAMILY WAY

Jane Robinson

Only a generation or two ago, illegitimacy was one of the most shameful things that could happen in a family. Today, babies' parents are as likely to be unmarried as married. This revolution in public opinion makes it easy to forget what it was like to give birth, or be born, out of wedlock in the years between the First World War and the dawn of the permissive age. In the Family Way tells secrets kept for entire lifetimes; in it we hear long-silent voices from the workhouse, the Magdalene Laundry, and the distant mother-and-baby home. Anonymous childhoods are recalled, spent in the care of Dr Barnardo or a child migration scheme halfway across the world. There are sorrowful stories — but also stories of hope, of triumph and the everyday strength of the human spirit.

YOUNG WINSTONE

Ray Winstone and Ben Thompson

Ray Winstone's amazing talent for bringing out the humanity buried inside his often brutal screen characters — violent offender in *Scum*, wife-beater in *Nil By Mouth*, retired blagger in *Sexy Beast* — has made him one of the most charismatic actors of his generation. But how do these uncompromising and often haunting performances square with his off-duty reputation as the ultimate salt-of-the-earth diamond geezer? The answer lies in the East End of his youth: the home of gangsters, bank robbers, Bobby Moore, and family and friends who looked out for each other . . .

NOT MY FATHER'S SON

Alan Cumming

Alan Cumming's father was the dark, enigmatic heart of Cumming family life — a man who meted out violence with frightening ease. But he was not the only mystery. Alan's maternal grandfather, Tommy Darling, had disappeared to the Far East after the Second World War. When Alan's mother was thirteen, the family was informed that he had died in an accidental shooting. Curious to explore this second mystery, Alan committed to filming an episode of the BBC's *Who Do You Think You Are?*. Then out of the blue his father, whom neither he nor his brother had spoken to for more than a decade, called. He had a secret to share — one that would shock his sons to the very core, and set in motion a journey that would change Alan's life forever.

THE DISINHERITED

Robert Sackville-West

In the small hours of the morning of 3 June 1914, a woman and her husband were found dead in a sparsely furnished apartment in Paris. It was only when the identity of the couple was revealed in the English press a fortnight later that the full story emerged. The man, Henry Sackville-West, had shot himself minutes after the death of his wife from cancer; but Henry's suicidal despair had been driven equally by the failure of his claim to be the legitimate son of Lord Sackville and heir to Knole. *The Disinherited* reveals the secrets and lies at the heart of an English dynasty, unravelling the parallel lives of Henry's four illegitimate siblings, one of whom secured a judicious marriage, while the other three were consigned to lives of poverty and disappointment.